GOD'S GONNA
Make You Laugh

GOD'S GONNA
Make You Laugh

Understanding God's Timing for Your Life

Noel Jones

DESTINY IMAGE® PUBLISHERS, INC.
P.O. Box 310, Shippensburg, PA 17257-0310

"Speaking to the Purposes of God for this Generation and for the Generations to Come."

This book and all other Destiny Image, Revival Press, Mercy Place, Fresh Bread, Destiny Image Fiction, and Treasure House books are available at Christian bookstores and distributors worldwide.

For a U.S. bookstore nearest you, call
1-800-722-6774.

For more information on foreign distributors, call
717-532-3040.

Or reach us on the Internet:
www.destinyimage.com.

ISBN 10: 0-7684-2317-1

ISBN 13: 978-0-7684-2317-4

For Worldwide Distribution, Printed in the U.S.A.

1 2 3 4 5 6 7 8 9 10 11 / 09 08 07

Contents

Foreword

I live in Los Angeles, California, but for five years worked in Washington, D.C., as host of a nightly television talk show on Black Entertainment Television (BET). During that five-year period, every Monday morning I would catch American Airlines flight #77 to Washington Dulles Airport (IAD) arriving just in time for my live show, and most every Friday morning, I would catch American Airlines flight #144 back to Los Angeles airport (LAX).

Countless times during that five-year period, I was asked why I didn't just move to D.C., why I'd return to Los Angeles every weekend racking up millions of frequent flier miles. My answer was always the same. In a word, well two, actually: "Noel Jones." Bishop Noel Jones is, in my estimation, without equal on the circuit of today's prophetic witnesses. Then again, I suspect that's exactly what most parishioners think about their pastor. But here's what makes me right; and most of the other powerful and prophetic preachers will second my motion. Jones has *style and substance*. They know it and many try to emulate it. Two funny stories to prove my point:

I once heard a preacher in Dallas tell of how he always wanted to work the mic(rophone) like Jones does when he's getting his *hoop* on. He moves the mic back and forth in a quick motion while he leans back and simultaneously puts his hand behind his ear while the organist follows him as he changes keys, hooping up the scale, and the audience is gone. Completely gone! Now that...that's style. Except when this preacher in Dallas tried it, he busted himself in the mouth with the mic—blood gushing everywhere. While Jones was pleading the blood, the other guy was bleeding the blood! Style!

But what's style without substance? Not much more than sounding brass and tinkling cymbal.

The substance of Jones's messages is already *legendary*—and I don't use that word lightly.

Consider this:

Some years ago Jones arrived in a city in Texas to preach a three-day revival. The pastor of the local church picked him up at the airport and, during the ride to the church, casually asked Bishop Jones what he intended to preach that night. Jones told him. The pastor then encouraged him to preach something else because the pastor had just preached that one a few Sundays prior! So Bishop Jones suggested another sermon. "Nope! Already did that too," the preacher responded. Well, it turned out that this preacher (like many others) gets Noel's tapes and, shall we say, "repurposes" them. His substance is so substantial, his hermeneutics so tight, his insight so keen, and his observations so interestingly unusual, that young preachers everywhere want to be like him...down to the suits and matching handkerchiefs. What a compliment! They say that imitation is the greatest form of flattery. But there's only one "First Noel," if you know what I mean. Often imitated, but never duplicated!

Because of his leadership, our church, the City of Refuge, was about to become the City of *Refuse*. That is to say that unless we built something quick, we were going to continue having to turn folks away. Nowhere to park. Nowhere to sit. Nowhere to stand. And that's no way to treat folks who are trying to find a little heaven after catching hell all week long.

So Jones says to me, "Ahhh, Tavis, we have a problem." I said, "Yes, and it's all your fault." He smiled. "But what a great problem to have—being one of the fastest growing churches in America." Which leads to my final thought...

At the moment, Noel Jones is still the best-kept secret in the Church. But not for long. More books, more television, more exposure. Don't be the last to discover the *preacher's preacher*: Noel Jones. Hear him, see him, read him, enjoy him, and then pass him on...for the Kingdom.

I feel sorry for folks like that young preacher in Texas who "repurposed" Jones's text. In just a little while, it's going to be hard, really hard, to do that and not get caught.

Keep the faith!

—Tavis Smiley
Los Angeles, California
June 15, 2005

Introduction

For more than 30 years, I have had the distinct privilege of traveling around the United States, the Caribbean, Europe, and Africa preaching the gospel of His Kingdom, a gospel that sets people free from the bondages of legalism, archaic religious thought, and the culturally oppressive systems of this world. In my travels, I have come to realize that no matter where I preach, people seem to share the same desires and have strikingly similar needs. For example, one of the most prevalent needs I encounter is that people want to be loved and conversely want to love others. If someone is deprived of love, the consequences of that deprivation can be quite drastic. Benjamin Disraeli, a 19th-century British novelist and politician, wrote that we are all born for love. It is the basic principle of human existence, and its only end. I am not surprised that this is one of the great needs of our times.

Besides the emotional need for love we are all confronted with the other basic needs of life: clothing, shelter, and food. These needs are often taken for granted here in the Western world. These are all obvious needs to us, ones that can be readily identified. Although these are basic needs of all humanity and should not be minimized, I have been on a search for most of my life, looking for the less obvious needs and concerns of people, the less obvious needs of humankind. Identifying and resolving the physical needs of people is not as much of a challenge as identifying and resolving the emotional, mental, and spiritual needs of the individual. These needs lay hidden beneath our consciousness, buried in the depths of our soul.

These "not so obvious" requirements for successful living are the ones that are most often neglected, resulting in a life that is spiritually, emotionally, and mentally deficient. If abused or neglected they will result in the starvation of the soul, leading to an emaciated and empty life. As I sat down to write this book, I was aware of the fact that there are thousands of books being published every day dealing with every subject imaginable. In looking for the right starting point there was a question continuously echoing in my spirit: "What do people *really* need?" Many thoughts began to emerge from my inner soul. We live in a world abounding with need, where much is promised (politically and spiritually) but little is delivered. Many people crowd their life with things they don't really need. "What do people *really* need?"

The Power in a Laugh

You might find this strange, but what kept coming to my mind was: laughter. I am sure that few preachers or psychologists would put this on their list. But those who interact with the world, like actors and musicians, know that laughter is an elixir for the wounded soul. Bob Newhart, the actor and comedian, once commented that laughter gives us distance. It allows us to step back from an event, deal with it, and then move on. Jimmy Buffett, Mr. Margaritaville, said that if we couldn't laugh, we would all go insane.

Most of the world does not live in Margaritaville. Most people live lives that are filled with moments of deep depression and pain, where laughter is a *luxury*. Laughter seems to be reserved for the king and his court while those outside the castle walls have never discovered a reason to laugh. Our culture is filled with a pressure and pain that impinges on our ability to find any joy in life.

I believe too many have forgotten the tremendous healing power of laughter. Laughter has always been a source of healing, accessible to the richest of the rich and the poorest of the poor. Dr. Tracy Gaudet, one of the premier women's physicians in the country, recently joined *The Oprah Winfrey Show* as part of the Lifestyle Makeover team. Dr. Gaudet focuses on showing women how busy, stressful lives can cause illness. She goes on to say that scientists have discovered that laughter helps your immune system fight the invasion of viruses and cancers. It lowers blood levels of the stress hormone cortisol and can lower your blood pressure and decrease heart strain. [1]

Other research reveals that laughter helps the cardiovascular system by giving the heart and lungs an aerobic workout and can reduce stress by helping to relax muscles. Hospitals have found that therapeutic humor stimulates the release of endorphins, the body's own pain relievers, and can decrease the average hospital stay by two days![2]

Mark Twain once said, *"Against the assault of laughter nothing can stand."*[5] What is the power of laughter? What is there about laughing that cures the aching heart? Like other emotional responses, laughing is a reaction that is stimulated by something humorous. However, when laughter is eliminated we can no longer see the comedy of life that is often played out right before our very eyes. We become blinded by our pain. But when we are able to tap into the humorous side of life, the erupting laughter becomes a mighty healing stream.

God—The Author of the Great Story

Consider how powerful that same force (the force of laughter) would be if God Himself were the one causing the laughter to erupt! Now I'm not saying that God is a cosmic comedian. He doesn't strut across the stage of life, delivering stomach-splitting one-liners. But our God is good for a great story—funny stories that are often birthed in tragedy and hardship! A story with an unexpected twist! Life is filled with these comedic stories created by the favor of the Father: the one voted least likely to succeed in life, becomes a successful businessman; the one who grew up in poverty ascends to a life of extraordinary achievement; the one lying at the doorway to death is visited by God and experiences His healing power. All because of a word! Well, not just any word: God's Word.

God—a comedian? A comedic God does not fit within our paradigm. Our image of God, fashioned in the despair of the Dark Ages, is the Angry God and not the Happy God. That image needs to change.

When you come to realize that the very person who is the main character in God's narrative is actually you, you will get my point. I don't mean that you are the brunt of some cosmic joke, but you sometimes have to laugh when God starts to awaken you from a bad dream and starts talking. The things that He says often do not make any sense at all, at least, not to the natural man. God tends to make some pretty lofty promises to His children. He loves to make predictions that cannot possibly come to pass under normal circumstances. Unless He does it, it just isn't going to happen!

We live in a day when life's challenges seem to be at an all-time high, but I know that God is still passing out promises to anyone *foolish* enough to freely receive them. His promises not only offer healing for the hurting, but they will reveal Him as the extraordinary God that He is—the laughing God who loves to turn our tragedy into triumph. As tough as things might appear right now, it is these dark times in your life that charge the atmosphere with the word of God. At these times He makes things that are impossible to become the possible. He is waiting for you to come to the revelation that He is faithful; no matter *what* your situation may look like, He is always there preparing a way for you.

Learning to See From God's Perspective

God lives in the realm outside of time, and when His word penetrates our world that is controlled by time, His words sometimes appear rather ridiculous, far-fetched. But it is all a matter of *perspective*. You cannot see the end of all things, but God can, and from His heavenly outlook He declares your future. You call His perspective ridiculous and crazy, but that is because you do not have eyes to see the invisible.

Perhaps you have suffered a recent loss or you've gone through a traumatic divorce. Maybe you've experienced the premature death of a child, or the tragic and sudden death of a loved one, or maybe you just lost all of your earthly possessions in bankruptcy court. Perhaps your house may have been destroyed by some catastrophic natural disaster such as a mudslide, tornado, or hurricane. To your utter disbelief, you discover that your homeowners insurance had lapsed just one month prior to the disaster, and now you have no idea how you will ever recover from the loss.

You may have been diagnosed with an incurable disease and given only a few months to live. Many of you have lived for many years never attaining anything of real value, or it seems that you have never tapped into your greatest potential. You may have given up all hope and thrown in the towel, calling it quits. You see nothing funny about your story, nothing to give you any reason to laugh. From your human position, life is not a comedy; it is a tragedy.

The Promise, the Process, and the Provision

But whatever your situation may be at this moment in time, *God's Gonna Make You Laugh*. This book was written to you—to give you hope—hope in the God who knows your future as well as your past. My goal is to lift you up to a higher place where you might come to see things from God's perspective and in that place you will learn to laugh. I am going to take you on a journey that starts with a ridiculous *promise*, goes through a challenging *process*, and finally brings you into the *provision* of all you have ever hoped for.

We will begin our journey with the story of an aged couple, Abraham and Sarah, who received a ridiculous promise from God. He told them He was going to bless them with a child from their withered old bodies. Kind of crazy, you might think. I will prove to you over and over again that trusting in God will *always* reward you with greater blessings than your mind could ever conceive. Not only that, I will also prove to you that all of the pain that you have gone through, or may presently be dealing with, will not last forever but will come to an end. The wait will be worth it all, contrary to what the enemy may be speaking to you right now.

I'm going to show you God's faithfulness. God is far more eager and able than I am to prove His own faithfulness to you. In fact, I have a sneaky suspicion that God has already proven Himself to you as a faithful Father, which is probably why you are reading this book. This book is not just about faith. It's far deeper than that. This book is about a promise, one that cannot be broken. And it is not about just any promise, but *the* promise. The promise will restore the joy of laughter to your life.

He is always present, always speaking to your spirit, reminding you that your life was intended for something bigger. You are a vehicle for His glory and not simply stuck in the status quo. Your life is much greater than you have realized up to this point in time, which is exactly why God has purposed for you to read this book. Within these pages you will see proof that God's promises *have* to come to pass. There is no way around it. You will discover that reservoir of spiritual resources that your Father has reserved just for you.

This blessing is a character issue with God, one that He takes very seriously, but it is connected to your faith and your patience. The discovery and realization of the promise is a *process*. What you must come to learn is that the reward at the end of the process will be so great that you will live the rest of your life in total amazement at the wondrous work of the Lord.

You may not be inclined to laugh right now while you are going through this present darkness. Believe me, I fully understand. But I promise you that laughter is on the horizon. It's coming! After all has been said and done, not only will God make you laugh, but others will laugh as well, when they see how God has blessed you in the most absurd ways. There is laughter, a hilarious eruption of joy, waiting for you.

Chapter 1

It's Your Time

To every thing there is a season, and a time to every purpose under the Heaven: A time to be born, and a time to die; a time to plant, and a time to pluck up that which is planted; a time to kill, and a time to heal; a time to break down, and a time to build up; a time to weep, and a time to laugh; a time to mourn, and a time to dance (Ecclesiastes 3:1-4 KJV).

Your time is limited, so don't waste it living someone else's life. Don't be trapped by dogma—which is living with the results of other people's thinking. Don't let the noise of other's opinions drown out your own inner voice. And most important, have the courage to follow your heart and intuition. They somehow already know what you truly want to become. Everything else is secondary. [4]

—Steve Jobs, CEO, Apple Computers

Before we move forward, it is important that you understand that the promise of success is right *now* and for *you*. I understand that I have given you a glimpse of your journey from its end rather than from its beginning. I may have spoiled the surprise, but knowing the end of the journey will give you courage during your journey. We all have a tendency to be *waiting* for God's promises rather than *working* toward those promises. Why should we waste precious time waltzing around our living room hoping for some miracle to happen? The rewards at the end are determined by our commitment to the process of reaching those rewards. That commitment will require work, patience, courage, pain, creativity, effort, and laughter.

Laughter is a key to enduring the process and reaching your goals. It is one of the most dynamic of the positive attributes, and it flows from your inner soul. I am not saying that there will not be tears and disappointment. What I am saying is that we must embrace the highs and the lows as we recognize the joy of life under any conditions. Martin Buber elaborates, in his *Tales of the Hasidim*, that the core of Hasidic teachings is the concept of a life of fervor, of exalted joy. [5] The Jews, a people who have probably suffered more than any other people in the history of the world, have learned to alleviate their sorrow with laughter.

"Better to laugh than to cry," says an old Yiddish proverb. While Jews account for less than 2.5% of the USA's population, approximately 70% of the USA's working comedians are Jewish: Mel Brooks, the Marx Brothers, Woody Allen, Milton Berle, Jerry Lewis, Jerry Seinfeld, Billy Crystal, Gilda Radnor, Jon Stewart, Weird Al, Jack Benny, George Burns, and many others. [6]

Action and Reaction

Some of God's promises are unconditional. An unconditional promise means that God determines that He is going to act in a certain way, and He does it. But most of His promises are conditional. God says, "If you do this, then I will do that." It's all about action and reaction. Unfortunately, many have become addicted to outside stimuli to encourage them, motivate them, and baby them. They become automatons marching to the beat of religious incentives and can find no interior stimuli to motivate them through the pain of life's obstacles.

You need to know how to respond to the sound of God; that's a healthy thing. And, conversely, God *has* to respond to your cry for help. This is the law of spiritual gravity. What goes up will certainly come down! You are not alone in your battles. There is a supernatural force that is available to you as you seek to reach your destiny.

But one of the keys to success is in how you respond to what is given you. It is not enough to have a promise. You have to act on that promise. There is God's part, and then there is your part. For every divine action, there must be a human reaction. One evening while King Solomon was asleep he heard these words: *"If My people, which are called by My name, shall humble themselves, and pray, and seek My face, and turn from their wicked ways; then will I hear from Heaven, and will forgive their sin, and will heal their land"* (2 Chron. 7:14 KJV).

Our actions create a response in the earthly and the heavenly realm. When we are faced with insurmountable problems, we can respond in one of two ways. We can look at the problem and shrink back in panic and perplexity, or we can forge ahead with courage and confidence. There is an enemy who seeks to block your pathway and keep you from reaching your personal God-given assignment. This enemy seeks to convince you that your time will *never* come. He creates illusions of delays and denials trying to convince you that God doesn't care. You must ignore his little tricks and understand that God *does* care and that He is working with you to make your dreams come true.

This enemy realizes that if he can successfully convince you that the day of promise will never come, then he knows that this unbelief will paralyze you with fear and cause you to slip into a spiritual dormancy. The only thing that will guarantee your failure is quitting. Those who win in this life are not those who never fail. Winners are those who never quit. Habakkuk, one of the great prophets of Israel, coined these words, *"For the vision is yet for the appointed time; it hastens toward the goal, and it will not fail. Though it tarries, wait for it; for it will certainly come, it will not delay"* (Hab. 2:3 NASB). In a similar vein of thought, Solomon, the builder of the Jewish temple, added these words, *"Hope deferred maketh the heart sick: but when the desire cometh, it is a tree of life"* (Prov. 13:12 KJV).

Once you give up to despair and give up to disappointment, you're done. It's over! No matter how difficult your circumstance may appear, you must realize that whatever comes, will come to *pass*—not to stay! Nothing remains forever. Not the good times and certainly not the bad times. Life is a river, and as you travel down that river you will encounter times of failure and disappointment, but there will also be times of great success. Triumph comes to those who have learned to wait and to endure and press forward into their future. Douglas MacArthur, one of the great generals in American history, once said that age wrinkles the body but quitting wrinkles the soul.

The process of waiting and enduring qualifies you for the next step—the step into your destiny. This process will take you out of your debt. It will alleviate you from those deteriorating and debilitating relationships. The divine promise is your guiding light and the anchor of your soul preventing you from succumbing to the temptation to give up right when you are so close to stepping over to the other side.

Belief Determines Actions

What you believe is very important. If you base your life on the belief of negative and false information, then it will affect who you are and what you do. Your life is the sum total of what you have believed up until this point. Too many people have based their life upon the negative information fed to them by parents, siblings, teachers, friends, and even preachers. This bad information has led to a life of sorrow and shame.

The first step to a new life is to delete all the old negative thought and injurious actions and begin to upload into your spirit new information based upon the truth of God's Word. God's truth about who you are and what your destiny is will set you free from emotional blindness, a spirit of poverty, negative speech, and rejection.

This new information will empower you to become a winner and not a quitter. It will give you a new set of eyes for the future and the destiny that awaits you. You will begin to understand that life is not based upon a welfare system. It is not based upon what others can give you but what you can create for yourself as you are willing to embrace the process that will guide you to success.

John Locke said that it is one thing to show a man that he is in an error, and another to put him in possession of truth. It is easy to point out people's faults. They are always so obvious. But this will never change the person. Better to put the truth in their hands. By the power of truth a life will change.

In order to be empowered by the truth you have to understand the difference between facts and truth. Truth is the sum total of the facts. The fact is that you have failed in life. The truth, however, is that you are not a failure. As poet Maya Angelou once wrote, "There's a world of difference between truth and facts. Facts can obscure the truth." [7]

Far too many Christians allow the facts to obscure the truth. They think that the fact that they are in the midst of a trial means that they have failed. They don't understand the truth that the road that leads to blessing sometimes—often—goes through valleys and dark places. They don't understand the *truth* that right *now* is your time.

The enemy had a plan to eliminate you and to confuse you with a pile of irrelevant facts. One of the many reasons why he could not kill you is because you had not yet received your promise. Once you have matriculated through this "School of Hard Knocks and Spiritual Development," the truth is that the promise given so long ago will become a reality.

The Theology of Time

Theology in its narrow sense is the study of God and His relationship with humanity and the world. Time is simply a period in which something exists, existed, or continues on. Hence the theology of time is the study of God and His relationship with humanity and the world—as it relates to time. Why does that matter at all? It does matter because before you can accurately understand God's season or why things happen the way they do, you must first realize that God has created time as a means to introduce His revelation to mankind. Once upon a time God....

God enters our world through revelation. Now I realize that what I've just said stands in direct contradiction to what many others teach on this subject. Many believe that they have the ability to choose when revelation comes to them from God. Or they'll say, "I need a revelation from the Lord, so let me go and get one." Although that may sound really spiritual, I'm not sure that it makes much biblical sense. If we are the ones who control the "time" issue, that means that God is man's maître d' waiting to serve him at his beck and call. We become the master and God becomes the servant. Listening to most people's prayers, this is exactly what God has become.

That is not how God's timing works. I cannot appoint myself as the next candidate for His next revelation. In fact, there is really not much that I can do to be chosen by Him. If I were able to put myself in the position to be qualified or competent, and think that somehow I can influence God at any time, then I would be acting on a false premise that God will reveal His thoughts to me based on my personal or spiritual merit. My merit has nothing to do with God's timing. Timing is based upon His grace, that is, His undeserved favor. In fact, God loves to choose the less deserving in order to manifest His glory.

Do you realize what a mess life would be, and how grossly unfair, if revelation were based on merit? In short, the rich, the intellectuals, the elite, and of course the pious clerics would be the only ones receiving God's revelation. That would not be just. And God is and always will be a just God! You have only to look at the life of Jesus to see how God operates. Jesus delivers His words to the *least* and the *last*, to those who live on the outer fringes of the religious and secular culture. Jesus was the king of one-liners, and these spiritual aphorisms centered on those that He chose to reveal Himself. "The last shall be first." "The least are the greatest in the Kingdom." Jesus had a way of turning the religious world upside down.

Humanism has taught us that we are the masters of our own fate and creators of our own destiny. That insidious philosophy has penetrated our religious souls so that we begin to think that we really have something to do with God's process of selection. I hate to be the bearer of bad news. The truth is that you have absolutely nothing to do with that at all. God chooses whom He pleases. It is all based on His sovereign will and amazing grace.

There are at least two kinds of people in the world. There are those who think that they can manipulate God and those who think that God would never choose them. "If it's all based on His sovereign will, then will He ever notice me amidst the billions of people in the world?"

That is a question worthy of an answer. Because it could seem that the world is one enormous lottery scheme in which

God hands out lottery tickets to all, and with one scratch of the finger some are chosen and others are rejected. Most people feel like they will never get selected. They have had bad luck all their lives. That may be what it seems like to you, but that is not how God works. Your life is not in the hands of fate and chance as the Greeks believed. God is bigger than that. And in His theology of time, looking at things from His judicial and gracious perspective, every single person has a destiny, a wonderful future determined by a loving God. I am not talking about Heaven. I am not referring to the "sweet bye and bye." I am talking about "right here and now."

God has designed a life of fulfillment and pleasure that looks nothing like the hell that has encompassed your life. He has created you with a unique style with a particular purpose. There is no evolutionary, random order to God's purpose. There is only a powerful design that is being worked out by God in your life!

So His system is nothing like the lottery where your life is controlled by the fate of purchasing the right ticket. That's hype. In God there is *no* hype; it's all real!

Anticipation—One of the Great Joys of Life

Time works in your favor, particularly when you know for sure that even if it's not today, your day *will* come—*guaranteed*. Your day will come, and you will have everything—everything you need to be successful and to fulfill your destiny.

One of the reasons I believe God set it up this way is so that we would trust Him and learn that all good things come to those who wait. Anticipation is one of the great joys of life. It brings focus and creates desire. Samuel Smiles, the 18th-century Scottish author, said that an intense anticipation itself transforms possibility into reality; our desires being often but precursors of the things which we are capable of performing.[8] Anticipation is a great motivator and drives the human soul toward its anticipated end.

But if we controlled our own destiny and could demand from God whatever we wanted, then we would have eliminated the power of anticipation. How would you ever develop genuine faith in Him, if you knew that He had to do whatever *you* say?

God does not work like that. He created time; man did not. God has all the time in the world. Time was created for His purposes, and He uses time to bring forth His destiny in your life.

Although He is not constrained or limited by time, in another sense, God has got all the time in the world. He is never in a hurry. And since He intuitively knows when it is the right time for sorrow to be turned into joy, He will wait until that time comes. It will come. It always does. The process of waiting creates the desired anticipation so that when it comes we will be able to better appreciate the treasure. We can only appreciate the miracle of the sunrise if we have lived through the dark night of the soul.

Waiting causes a refinement of our priorities and a sharpening of our vision and a shaping of our souls. When we first receive the promise we do not have clear priorities, sharp vision, or the character to contain the gift. Time is a tester. Whatever endures the test of time will stand. Time is a creator. Within the context of time, lives are created and success is achieved.

Understanding God's Time

Some things will never come to us until it is time, especially the things that God wants to give us. Timing is everything. If you allow impatience to rule and seek to bypass God's timing, there will be disastrous results. Just ask Abraham. The present state of life in the Middle East is the result of one man seeking to get the promise his way. If you were to be honest with yourself, you would admit that some of your past failures are the result of running ahead of God's time and pursuing things when you were not ready for those things. I admit that I have prematurely entered into relationships that would have succeeded and had healthier results if I had only waited for the *right* season.

Saint Augustine said that patience is the companion to wisdom. Patience is not a common trait of the human species and especially of us living in the Western world. With all of our technologies, we are geared for instant access, instant service, and instant messaging. In God's world, it doesn't work that way and that is why so many people are struggling.

Many people enter into marriage without ever considering if this was the right person and if the timing was right. Drifting along on the sea of our emotions and allowing those emotions to determine our lives have led many people down a blind alley. And when that happens, it clearly spells—*disaster!* We can't expect to make solid decisions based on our emotions, particularly since they are so volatile. Patience produces wisdom. It gives us the time to accurately think through our decisions. It allows time for God to invade our thought processes. Until we learn this truth we will continue to miss the mark and prolong the process.

But when the fullness of the time was come, God sent forth His Son, made of a woman, made under the law, to redeem them that were under the law, that we might receive the adoption of sons (Galatians 4:4-5 KJV).

Fullness of time—at the right time, when it was most propitious and advantageous, God entered into our world in the person of Christ. It is interesting that Jesus Christ did not enter into the earth realm in a physical sense until it was time. He was desperately needed long before He was born. If we had been the judges of time, we would have sent Him a lot sooner. The Bible tells us that Sodom was an increasingly wicked city. *"But the men of Sodom were wicked and sinners before the Lord exceedingly"* (Gen. 13:13 KJV). They were so wicked that God could not even find two handfuls of people who were living righteous lives within that entire region. It was obvious that Jesus was needed *then*. But God waited. There was a future time that would be more perfect than that time. When everything lined up perfectly, then He was sent into our world.

Just because it doesn't happen *today* does not mean that it *won't* happen. It's just not time! All of life confirms the truth of time. An embryo has to go through a nine-month gestation period in its mother's womb before it can be born with the best possibility of perfect health with the least chance of complications. Now a baby can be born at six or even five months and live. However, it will often have to undergo special treatment to correct what should have occurred in the womb. In a premature birth, the newborn's brain, organs, and even limbs can be underdeveloped, necessitating medical treatment to strengthen those weak body parts. That newborn baby is often labeled a "preemie" or premature baby because it has not completed the full cycle pre-ordained to ensure the right time for delivery. Growth is not instantaneous; it happens within the womb of time.

When you try to rush your *due* time, you will end up losing time and then will have to play catch up. Solomon articulated it well when he said that to *everything* there is a time and a season. The converse is true. When your time comes, nothing can stop it. When it's *your* time, there is *nothing* that can stop that promise from coming forth!

The story of Lazarus, recorded in John 11, establishes this truth. One day Jesus got word that His good friend, Lazarus, was dying. Lazarus' sisters, Mary and Martha, were begging Him to come. His disciples thought that He would leave immediately. To their consternation, He did not. His disciples didn't get it. "There is a need, so why aren't You going to him?" Jesus waited till Lazarus had died. This makes no sense. Jesus had the power to heal His friend but waited till he died. This sounds like *bad* timing.

Jesus appeared to be totally insensitive to Mary and Martha's feelings. Mary, Martha, and Lazarus were dear and close friends of Jesus. Whenever Jesus would travel through their town on His way to a particular region, He would always stop off at their home and eat and hang out there with them. He was comfortable in their presence and loved them so much.

Not only were they His friends, they were also believers. Why is that so important? It was dangerous to be associated with Jesus because of His controversial ministry. People were calling Him "Messiah" and many were following Him, much to the chagrin of the religious leaders. They were always watching to see who was hanging out with this guy. Most people realized that their lives would be in great jeopardy by merely listening to and agreeing with His teachings. Yet these sisters loved Him so much and believed in Him so unwaveringly that they *knew* that if Jesus were there even seconds before their brother's death that He would be able to heal him. How could He not answer their cry for help?

I believe Jesus must have been as grieved as Mary and Martha as He contemplated the crushing disappointment that His friends must be feeling at His seeming indifference to Lazarus' need. *Their* hurt and pain became *His* hurt and pain. This was the only time that we see recorded that Jesus wept. He might have wept, not only because He felt their grief, but because they did not understand the times and seasons of the Father. They did not realize that whenever God shows up, it is always *the right time*. It is impossible for God to be late!

God had a better plan. Remember that God does not operate in our realm of minutes, hours, days, weeks, and years. He exists outside of time. The disciples lived in an earthly dimension and could not see that plan. When Jesus raised Lazarus from the dead they finally understood that Father knows best.

God's Time—The Fifth Dimension

In the same way, Father knows what is best for your life. God is waiting for some things to die in you before He will show up with a miracle. There can be no resurrection until there is a death. That is part of the process. His delays are not denials. They are simply a part of the process of preparation so that you are ready to enjoy what God is going to bring into your life.

Between the promise and the fulfillment you will walk through the valley of the shadow of death. The reason for this is that God will not reveal Himself in the season that *you* think is best. The God that lives above and beyond time is the one that understands the proper time for your rescue, your healing, your blessing, and your victory.

God's time is not our time, but it is the right time. Timing is a *vision* thing. We cannot see from His point of view. Our vision is obstructed by our placement in this time/space world. We live in a three-dimensional world including longitude, latitude, and altitude. We cannot exist in two places at the same time. Einstein defined time as the fourth dimension. God, however, lives in another dimension that is not controlled by longitude, latitude, or altitude and is unhindered by clocks and calendars. He lives outside of time but chooses to work within time. His time is the fifth dimension. It is another time that He controls.

He can make the sun to shine in the middle of the winter, the snow to fall in spring, and rain to pour in the middle of autumn, and He can cause a good old nor'easter cold front to come blowing through the middle of a blistering hot August. The bottom line is, whenever He comes is the *right time* and the *right season*. When it's time for Him to come through on your behalf, nothing in the world will be able to stop the success that He has chosen for your life.

Time—An Enemy or a Friend

I am always amazed by the behavior of small children. If you promise a small child that you are going to take him in six months to Six Flags amusement park or to the zoo, then every day until that time arrives you will have to endure his insistent questionings and badgering. "When are we going to the zoo? Is it tomorrow? Next week? When? Please, please tell me."

Or if you are just going on a trip from Los Angeles to San Diego, as soon as you leave your driveway, make two lefts and a right onto the freeway, you hear the little backseat drivers asking, "Are we there yet?" Often our behavior is very much like little children in that respect. We make ourselves miserable while waiting for our promise to manifest. They have no concept of time. But neither do we.

Like the Rolling Stones sang, "Time is on my side." Time is actually your friend. Before you can understand this truth you have to recognize that within the time period between your promise given and your promise received, you can be engaged in the process of maturation. Many people miss this vital lesson and never actualize the full meaning and purpose of waiting within time. Jesus, the master storyteller, once told a story about wise and foolish virgins that illustrates this point.

*Then shall the kingdom of heaven be likened unto ten virgins, which took their lamps, and went forth to meet the bridegroom. And **five of them were wise,** and **five were foolish.** They that were foolish took their lamps, and took no oil with them: But **the wise took oil in their vessels** with their lamps. While **the bridegroom tarried, they all slumbered and slept.** And at midnight there was a cry made, Behold, the bridegroom cometh; go ye out to meet him. Then all those virgins arose, and trimmed their lamps. And the* *foolish said unto the wise, Give us of your oil; for our lamps are gone out. But the wise answered, saying, Not so; lest there be not enough for us and you: but go ye rather to them that sell, and buy for yourselves. And while they went to buy, the bridegroom came; and they that were ready went in with him to the marriage: and* **the door was shut** (Matthew 25:1-10 KJV, emphasis added).

Each one of these ten virgins had equal time and opportunity to do what needed to be done. They all had equal access. But the Bible tells us that five of them were wise, and five were foolish. The five that were foolish did not lack intelligence or business skills. They were not cognitively underdeveloped. What made them foolish was their poor utilization of the time allotted them. They were lazy in their waiting. They did not take advantage of the waiting time. They should have been working while they were waiting. They procrastinated. Procrastination is the enemy of time and results in lost opportunity.

You should never consider it a negative thing when you have to wait for God's promise to come to pass. During that period of time, you should be involved in the process that will lead you to the promise. They prepared for the moment when the groom would arrive. In our world this is also true. Too many women are looking for the right husband rather than focusing on becoming the right woman. Because these women are looking rather than preparing, many men pass them by. By the way, this applies to you men as well.

Countless numbers of Christians that I preach to all over this country sincerely desire to be wealthy. They believe that God has told them that they will have wealth and prosperity. Here is the problem. The word is good and true, but they make no preparation for the wealth that is on the way. During that *waiting period*, they could be getting out of debt, taking finance classes, reading books on finances, and attending investment workshops. But instead they choose to do nothing. When the money comes, it passes them right by—because success comes to those who have prepared for success. The time between the promise given and the promise received is *preparation time*. It is the time in which God wants to prepare us to handle the blessing that is coming our way.

The foolish virgins slept while the wise virgins worked. Had that been me, I would have ordered a few cups of coffee and expected to pull an *all-nighter*. There would be no way that I would allow my opportunity to pass me by, if I had anything to do with it.

I know that I said that God is sovereign and that He reveals Himself to whomever He chooses, but that does not preclude your involvement in making your dream come alive. Once the promise comes to you and once you have been given a vision for your life, you need to plan and prepare to enter into your dream. That is the purpose of waiting.

Time is a gift given to you by God for the purpose of preparation so that you can handle the success He wants to give you. Time was designed by the Father to be your friend, and it will be as long as you consciously choose to treat her with respect. If you abuse the time allotted to you, then you will shockingly discover that when you try to make your grand entry into your promise, **the door will be shut.** Don't make time your enemy.

In Time I Will Trust

Rather than despising time, you need to trust time. You need to use time for your benefit. Some people act as if God is on their timetable. They believe that God has to *prove* something to them before they will give Him their undivided loyalty. God does not have to prove *anything* to you. He has never broken His promises. Time is given for the purpose of developing trust in God. If you wait to trust God, you will miss God. You'll miss your appointment and therefore miss His directions.

Lack of trust will create further delays. They will not be God's delays. They will be delays created by your lack of trust in God. If you learn to trust Him, He will direct your life. He will provide a road map that will lead you to a place of great blessing and success. If you don't trust Him, He won't give you the road map. No road map, no progress. No progress, no promise. It's as simple as that. The more you *trust*, the more He *reveals* Himself in the midst of your waiting. Time is on your side if you learn to trust God while going through the process to the promise. As trust is being built, time will collapse, and the promise will become yours.

Chapter 2

It's All Part
of the Process

Education is the process in which we discover that learning adds quality to our lives. Learning must be experienced.[9]

—William Glasser, American Psychiatrist

Learning is the beginning of wealth. Learning is the beginning of health. Learning is the beginning of spirituality. Searching and learning is where the miracle process all begins.[10]

—Albert Einstein

Most people have a dream of the possibilities created by a prosperous life. They imagine the advantages that will come their way if they achieved those dreams. There is one problem. Most people fantasize about the rewards at the conclusion of the journey, overlooking the cost of the journey. Unfortunately, few people are willing to go through the process that will lead them to the fulfillment of their dreams.

Everybody wants to become the next great Bishop T.D. Jakes, Joyce Meyer, or Bishop Eddie Long, the next Oprah Winfrey or Jada Pinkett-Smith, Bill Gates, Denzel Washington, Will Smith, Venus or Serena Williams, Tavis Smiley, or Warren Buffett. Dreams are important, but if they are not followed up by a commitment to the process, then they will simply remain daydreams, never seeing the light at the end of the tunnel. If you are interested in fulfilling your destiny, then you must learn to view failure as a healthy, inevitable part of the process of success. Alex Noble once said that success is not a place at which one arrives, but rather the spirit with which one undertakes and continues the journey. The journey is the process. It cannot be avoided, for the process is part of the preparation that is needed to enter into and sustain success.

It is easy to look at those who have succeeded and wish that we could be like them. We like what they have, but I am not sure if we would like what they went through to get what they have. The one thing that is common to all successful people is that they were willing to endure the process that was necessary to reach their own dreams. You see the big homes they live in and the nice cars they drive. What you do not see is the pain, the rejection, the failure, the commitment, the labor, and the many hours dedicated to reaching their goals.

Their success was the result of hard work, discipline, risk taking, patience, and focus. It didn't just happen for them overnight.

There are always struggles and obstacles awaiting those who want to succeed in life.

If there is no struggle there is no progress.

—Frederick Douglas

The sacrifices involved in fulfilling your dreams can be exacerbating and, at times, debilitating. Sacrifice is part of the process. There will be opposition and obstacles. There will be failure and disappointment. They cannot be avoided; they must be conquered. I like what Leonardo da Vinci said about obstacles, "Obstacles cannot crush me; every obstacle yields to stern resolve."

You must start the journey understanding that no good thing comes without a price. As they say, "No pain, no gain." You must be willing to walk through the pain and rejection. You must understand that *failure is never final*; it is simply a part of the process on the journey.

Success is a journey, not a destination. The doing is usually more important than the outcome. Too many people are sitting around waiting for some miracle to drop in their lap. Success does not drop from the sky. Success is built by the labor of your hands and the passion of your heart. There is a process, a journey, involved in every new venture. Success is determined by how you overcome the obstacles, manage the mistakes, and resist the rejection. It is never instant.

Instant Success Is a Myth

The promise of instant success is a myth. There are few, if any, overnight successes in real life. Winning the lottery cannot be counted as instant success. The statistics of those who lost everything only a year or two after winning the lottery is staggering. The truth is that there is much that is learned in the process that will sustain you once you reach your goals. Living in the fantasy world of expecting instant success will be a great hindrance to reaching your desired dream.

No one makes it overnight and those that do usually fail. Why? Because they have never been trained to manage success, spend sensibly, and invest wisely. What invariably happens when they get their first real taste of money is really self-destructive. Because they have no plan on how to handle success, they end up losing what they gained.

Attitudes of the Successful

"If I could just get a new exotic car, a mansion, or if I had mad amounts of diamonds and gold jewelry, then I know I'd live happily ever after." Your motivation will determine your success. Money is not a goal. It is a byproduct of reaching your goal. Actors and actresses go to school, work hard, and take whatever job they can get along the way to reaching their goal. Their goal is in the movies, and money is the byproduct. An athlete will work in the gym, manage his diet, and work endlessly at developing his skill so that he can reach the NFL. The NFL is the goal, and money is the byproduct.

You must learn that money is not your motivation. That motivation will not carry you through the difficult times. Your contribution to society is your goal, and money simply becomes the reward of all of your hard labor. Successful people want to accomplish something in life. Their eyes are not on the luxuries that fame will bring them. Their eyes are on the goal of succeeding in life. They understand that wealth is the byproduct.

This is why it is dangerous to become rich overnight. You never had to work for that wealth. You never had a goal in mind. You were never focused on a particular dream. You never had to work, never had to save, never had to face failure, and you never had character built into you through the process.

What you gain overnight, you are bound to lose overnight. Although I believe that God can and often does get people out of debt overnight, it is not necessarily the best method for everyone. There are some things that you need to discover first about what actually got you into enormous debt in the first place. If you freely run up your personal debt by careless use of credit cards, you must learn that the way back is a long tedious road. It can be accomplished, but you must make sacrifices in order to reach the goal of getting out of debt. You need to understand what to *embrace* and what to *avoid*. You've got to learn when to buy and when to refrain from purchasing. It's called *process*.

Ask Oprah or Bill Gates or Denzel Washington or even Tiger Woods how they are enjoying their overnight success? If you read their stories you will discover that the journey to success was long and hard. You don't build an empire in a day. Winning the Masters was not a stroke of luck for Tiger Woods. As a young kid he lived under the discipline that his father provided. He spent hours, days and months and years stroking and putting the ball. While others were out playing, he was out working and perfecting his game.

Successful people make a *decision* about what they want to be. Then they are *determined* and *disciplined* in working toward their goal. They appreciate the process rather than despising the process.

The Process Creates Appreciation for Success

I've been preaching and traveling for the past 35 years. I know that may surprise you, but I started out real early in life. If I had possessed back then what I have now, it would have been disastrous. I would have been reckless and not responsible. I would not have an infrastructure set in place to be able to accommodate and appreciate what I have right now. The process helped me to have a greater appreciation for everything that I have.

It took time for me to be able to not only gain the wisdom that I have, but also appreciate the value of everything that God has given to me. When I was real young, it hadn't quite hit me yet. It took time for me to process that heavy information. But the process has made me better and helped me to appreciate all that I have. Did I enjoy the pain or the rejection? No! But I now understand that there is no success without heartache and failure. So many people try everything they can to avoid the process of life. They are looking for shortcuts to success. They don't understand that shortcuts will only lead you down dark alleys and dead ends. Look at those who get into dealing drugs. They have avoided the pathway of education and instead have chosen the quick fix (no pun intended). Most drug dealers are entrepreneurs and very smart people. They have simply chosen a dangerous shortcut to success—a shortcut that eventually leads to death or jail.

Unfortunately, they don't want to go through the process of becoming the skilled CEO's of major corporations, or entrepreneurs of their own businesses, or even designers. Many of them would be phenomenal pharmacists or even medical doctors. After all, they enjoy selling the stuff. But they view the process of going through years of college or applied training and study as not being worth the while, or even worth the wait. They have been sold on the life of "bling bling," financial riches, and security, but refuse to take the legal paths to arrive at that place. They see the cars, the houses, and the status, and then they want it overnight. The quick route is the more appealing way. Little do they realize that the quick route, the instant path, will only get them incarcerated somewhere in a lonely dark cell.

Great rappers and musicians go through a process before they arrive at their blessing. They have to practice long hours perfecting their skills and craft. In their early days they had to play on, sing on, or rap on every single show that was playing just to get exposure. They justified the time put in as "paying my dues." When you pay your dues you have a greater appreciation for the reward at the end of the rainbow. Many of them held down 9-5 jobs while they were pursuing their passion, having to care for the needs of their household. Some of them would make demo CD's in the studio and sell them out of the trunk of their cars at supermarkets, malls, movies theaters, churches, and wherever just to get some exposure.

The Pursuit of Happiness

A blockbuster movie recently released from Hollywood, *The Pursuit of Happyness*, illustrates my point perfectly. Will Smith played the real-life character, Chris Gardner. Chris Gardner in real life was an out-of-work salesman who wins custody of his young son just as he is about to start a new job. In the beginning all does not go well for Gardner in his pursuit of happiness. He ends up in a homeless shelter trying to look after his son. In 1983, he spent many nights in homeless shelters and sometimes lived on the streets. On some nights he and his son would crash at flop-houses or hole up in a far corner of Union Square. Bathing was often done in the sinks of public bathrooms. For meals, Gardner brought his son, then a toddler, to the soup kitchen at Glide Memorial Church. But he did not give up on his dream. It was there in that soup kitchen where he met the Rev. Cecil Williams. Williams let Gardner keep his son at the soup kitchen when he finally got a $1,000-a-month pay as a stock-broker trainee. He was eventually able to save enough money to put down a deposit on a rental house in Berkeley. Eventually Gardner would become an extremely wealthy man owning his own brokerage firm. He did not take the shortcut offered to him on the streets. He took the high and hard road that led to success.

In Order to Possess the Promise, You Have to Go Through the Process

What I am saying is that there is definitely a process that everyone has to endure in order to possess the promise. The question is: How badly do you really want it? What are you willing to go through in order to get what God said is yours? Is the journey even worth it to you, or is it just too laborious?

You must answer these questions honestly before you move forward. Because if the promise is really worth it to you, then you will be willing to go through the process gracefully, knowing that on the other end of your pathway through the wilderness is the promised land. Young preachers want to become like me overnight. While that may be somewhat flattering to me, it really does not make sense at all. If a person wants what I have, then they must first walk in my shoes. You must go through what I've gone through. It is not just about getting my tapes and listening to them and imitating what I do.

You may learn style and method that way, but you won't discover the lessons I learned that shaped my fundamental philosophy and fashioned my life. Although I am enrolled in the lifelong process of learning, and I read books, periodicals, magazines, and journals voraciously, there are still some things that I will only discover through experience. You may argue with my theology all day long, trying to write it off as inaccurate because you don't see things the way I see them. Or you may have been educated in a different stream of learning from me that may oppose what I've learned and how I've been trained. Our arguing on some fine point would be utterly foolish and most unproductive. But there is one thing that you cannot refute: my *testimony* that is derived from my *experience*.

The School of Experience

A man with an experience is never at the mercy of a man with an argument. My experience validates my ministry and my mission. One faces the future with one's past. You may have seminary or college education and have lots of degrees. These are wonderful things. However, they are no substitute for experience.

If I tell you that the Jesus of the Gospels healed the sick and raised the dead, you can argue that point till hell freezes over, if you don't believe in divine healing. On the other hand, if I tell you that Jesus healed *me* on my deathbed and raised me up to tell you about it, there is nothing substantial that you can say or do to rebut my claim.

Elbert Hubbard, an American writer and philosopher who died on the *Lusitania* when it was torpedoed and sunk by a German submarine, once wrote that God will not look you over for medals, degrees, or diplomas, but for scars. Experience is not about what happens to you. It is about what you do with what happens to you.

Experience creates a new vocabulary. It's through life's processes that we gather the experience that gives us something to talk about. Take that away and all you have is supposition. Add experience to your life and you have wisdom. Knowledge is power, but wisdom teaches you how to handle the power, and that wisdom can only come from experience. Without experience, all of our knowledge simply puffs us up and makes us appear larger than we really are.

It's not about the custom clothing, or the Louis Vuitton briefcase, or the alligator shoes. Those are just outward trappings that do not necessarily mean that you have anything to offer. Substance always trumps style. The real issue is what is in your soul, not what is in your bank account.

I want to know how you handled life when you had no money to replace those worn-out shoes. Tell me about the way you reacted to rejection and how you overcame all the impossibilities that were before you. I want to know the stories of when you had no suit, and now you own a clothing store. That's the process that you cannot avoid. It is all part of the *making* process, the process that prepares you for your reward.

Even Jesus Had to Endure His Process

Looking unto Jesus the author and finisher of our faith; who for the joy that was set before Him endured the cross, despising the shame, and is set down at the right hand of the throne of God (Hebrews 12:2 KJV).

One of the sobering things about "going through," in order to get where I have to go, is knowing that I am not the only one who has had to travel these paths. The paths that I travel are ancient paths. Somebody has walked this way before me. It is so refreshing to know that Jesus also had to go through a process in order to receive the reward of pleasing His Father and reconciling humanity back to the Father.

Hebrews 12:2 offers us a wonderful clue as to how Jesus was able to endure the most horrifying treatment and castigation of His life. Jesus Christ did no wrong. The Bible tells us that He was without sin, something that no one else on earth could ever lay claim to. *"For we have not an high priest which cannot be touched with the feeling of our infirmities; but was in all points tempted like as we are, yet without sin"* (Heb. 4:15 KJV). Despite the fact that He never committed wrong, He had to go through the process of having to bear the weight of the world's sin on His holy shoulders. He didn't pray for a lighter burden, but for a stronger back. *"For*

He hath made Him to be sin for us, who knew no sin; that we might be made the righteousness of God in Him" (2 Cor. 5:21 KJV).

In other words, He was sentenced for a crime that He never committed. How did He endure such a travesty? Most people would have snapped under those kinds of conditions. But Jesus lasted! He endured His process. The only way that He could do this was to constantly remind Himself of the joy associated with the reward on the other side of the pain. He had eyes to see the invisible. The Bible says, *"Who, for the joy that was set before Him, endured the cross"* (Heb. 12:2 KJV). This statement can at first seem like an oxymoron. How can you have joy enduring the enormous weight of a cross on your back, especially when you did nothing to deserve it? Only when you focus on the joy of having completed the mission will you be able to keep going forward.

How is it that so many Jewish people survived the horrible Holocaust when more than six million of their family and friends were murdered? What gave this remnant, the faithful few, that power to continue on despite seemingly impossible odds? They had to have known instinctively that the brightness of the promise on the other side of their persecution would somehow far outweigh the crushing darkness of the persecution itself.

If they had continued to look at the persecution, they would have been swallowed up by despair and hopelessness. Simply said, you have to stay focused on hope in order to make it through. Once you give up on hope, you've lost the battle and, with that, your joy to continue. Ultimately Jesus endured the cross because He knew that in the final analysis it would be worth it all. Keep hope alive!

Abraham's Prolonged Process

Abraham's story is the very source of inspiration for this work. There are so many things that we can learn from his example. One of the first things I want you to notice in this story is that Abraham laughed *too soon*. That's right! Don't laugh at God's word for you! As absurd as His promise may sound to you initially, you need to reevaluate and think it through before you respond foolishly. God never speaks about trivial and light matters; everything that He promises is always in the spectacular since that is the kind of God He is.

> *Then Abraham fell upon his face, and laughed, and said in his heart, Shall a child be born unto him that is an hundred years old? and shall Sarah, that is ninety years old, bear?* (Genesis 17:17 KJV).

The pathway to the promise requires endurance and hope. Endurance is the energy to press through all the obstacles on the journey. Hope is the vision that sees the end of the journey. Martin Luther King Jr. in *The Trumpet of Conscience*, wrote: "If you lose hope, somehow you lose the vitality that keeps life moving, you lose that courage to be, that quality that helps you go on in spite of it all. And so today I still have a dream."[11]

God told Abraham, at the ripe old age of 100, that he would have a son of promise. This same promise was given decades before that, but Abraham delayed its fulfillment because he could not accept the fact that God wanted to give him something that he had never had. Not only did God want to give Abraham and Sarah something that they had never had, but also He wanted to give them something that would literally defy the laws of nature. And since God's promise violated the natural order of things, they did not respond properly. They had no vision that could look beyond the natural. Rather than just believing and receiving the promise, they laughed. This was not the laugh of faith, but of disbelief. This was not the response God was looking for.

Never laugh at God when He wants to bless you beyond your wildest dreams. You live in an apartment complex, but God has promised that you'll own the entire complex *and* a mansion. Does that make you laugh? You may be a fifth generation welfare recipient, and God just said that you were going to own the largest supermarket chain in your state. Laugh out loud! Laugh in faith!

You never saw yourself as a wondrous creation of God, beautiful in every way, but rather viewed yourself as flawed and marred. Then God tells you that you are going to be the next Miss America. Yeah, I know you want laugh. You don't even own a bike, yet God wants to bless you with a Rolls Royce Phantom. It just doesn't make any sense at all.

The only response you may feel is to want to laugh at the perceived absurdity of the promise. As natural as that response may be, don't fall for it. It's the wrong comeback! Now it's one thing if your so-called friends and family members laugh at you. That's all right; they don't know any better. But believers should never laugh at what God wants to do in them and through them. That insults God. It says that He's not able to do what He says He will do.

God takes that real personal! When I was a child, we used to dream about owning this car or that car. Often one of my friends would say, "I'm getting this car," or "I'm going to buy this outfit," or "I am going to go out with that girl." If the car was an expensive one or if the outfit was an in-style outfit, or if the girl was fine, we'd immediately inform him, "You ain't getting nothin'! Yeah, right!"

What we were doing was discounting his ability to produce what he said he could, based on his character. Needless to say, he never produced anything. God is not like that. Regardless of how outlandish it sounds, if God says it then it *shall* come to pass. The impossible is simply what nobody has done till somebody does it. The impossible is always there waiting for that someone.

Don't laugh just yet, wait until the blessing arrives and then we will all laugh together in total amazement at the marvelous works of the Lord. Proper laughter is a matter of timing. It is a matter of laughing *at* God or laughing *with* God. The difference is huge. One is the laugh of doubt, and the other is the laugh of faith.

I will praise Thee: for Thou hast heard me, and art become my salvation. The stone which the builders refused is become the head stone of the corner. This is the Lord's doing; it is marvelous in our eyes (Psalm 118:21-23 KJV).

How Long Will You Have to Wait?

He giveth power to the faint; and to them that have no might He increaseth strength. Even the youths shall faint and be weary, and the young men shall utterly fall: But they that wait upon the Lord shall renew their strength; they shall mount up with wings as eagles; they shall run, and not be weary; and they shall walk, and not faint (Isaiah 40:29-31 KJV).

For many people the process is pure drudgery because of the *waiting time.* I know that it's not fun; it's no joyride. Nobody ever said it would be easy. Between the wish and the thing is the waiting.

But how long do you have to wait? *Keep waiting until you receive wisdom and learn the lesson associated with the journey.* For some folks, that may be longer than for others. You need to be able to answer the question, "What have you learned from all that you've been through?" If you can't answer that, then you may have to repeat the cycle all over again, making your wait even longer.

You must wait until you receive strength. At times life may deal you such a significant blow that it may appear that you are down for the count. Really all that you need is a chance to catch your breath, regroup, and regain your strength. Once that happens, you are ready to fight again.

And I've got good news for you! When you finally receive your promise after waiting and enduring, the process goes on! You will then have to stand your ground to *maintain* that which God has given to you. The enemy hates when you get rewarded, and he will do everything to try to steal your reward. It is then that you will need strength to guard and protect the anointing and the glory on your life. The only things that are really worth stealing are the things that are precious and highly valuable. Don't let the enemy steal what you have by tempting you to lose patience and take shortcuts.

Keep waiting until it no longer feels like you're waiting! *Run, and not be weary. Walk, and not faint.* Much like a marathoner, you need to pace yourself because the course is a long one. If you get tired too soon, you won't have the strength needed to complete the race. Benjamin Franklin once said that he who can have patience could have what he will. Patience is waiting. Not passively waiting—that is laziness. But to keep going when the going is hard and slow—that is patience.

Chapter 3

Where Are You Going?

By faith Abraham, when he was called to go out into a place which he should after receive for an inheritance, obeyed; and he went out, not knowing whither he went. (Hebrews 11:8 KJV)

Take the first step in faith. You don't have to see the whole staircase, just take the first step.

—Dr. Martin Luther King Jr.

The life of Abraham teaches us one vital lesson: It is possible to be in the will of God and yet not know where you are going. Typically, we would determine that if a person does not know where they are going, they would not be successful. One of the keys to success that is on everyone's list is to know your ultimate goal so that you plan on how you are going to reach it.

How can you be successful if you do not know where you are going?

I do believe that everyone in life has a purpose and that they should live their lives in constant pursuit of that purpose. To do anything less would be unacceptable for the fulfillment of your life. However, if one does not know where they are going that is not necessarily a bad thing. Sometimes God sets you on a course, and you don't necessarily know where it is going to take you. This is one of the mysterious ways that God interacts with humans. He only shows them the first step. The second step is your step of faith. God has this proclivity of not giving us the full directions for the journey. We don't always get all the directions beforehand.

At this point in his life, Abraham was a senior citizen. He was fairly secure in his life. He was settled and content. Yet God chose to unsettle Abraham's comfortable lifestyle. He told him to leave his family that he loved and go to a place. What place? Well, that was the challenge! He didn't tell him what place. He told him to get up, start moving, and then He would show him the place. Can you imagine his conversation with his wife and family? There wasn't much detail that he could give them. They probably thought he was crazy. One of the major obstacles to change is personal comfort. If we find ourselves in a comfortable place in life, it will be difficult to leave that place of comfort and embrace the enigmatic. I have learned that if you are going to walk with God, you must be willing to let go of what you have in order to lay hold of what He wants to give you.

Leaving the Comfort Zone

God always messes with our area of comfort—our *comfort zone*. It is not that God wants us to be uncomfortable, but rather that He wants us to take the journey that leads to higher altitudes—higher than we've ever dreamed we could go. But He knows that if we are satisfied with where we are now, we will never take the initiative to travel to areas that will stretch us and, through hard places, strengthen us. The person of faith must always be willing to relinquish the luxuries of life in order to respond to the lure of the unthinkable.

Let me say here that all trials are not necessarily related to the enemy. Often, we are called to encounter difficulties because these difficulties are part of the process of getting us from where we are at to where God wants us to be. An uncomfortable moment could simply be a moment in time when God is preparing you for the next giant step into your destiny.

Sometimes the challenging moments in life are an instant message from God that maybe where we *are* is not where we *should* be. Life can get painful when you choose to wait before you act on His Word. Hesitation can lead to unhappy places. Sometimes the pain is a way of waking us up. C.S. Lewis said it well when he wrote these words. "God whispers to us in our pleasures, speaks to us in our conscience, but shouts in our pains: It is His megaphone to rouse a deaf world."[12]

Let's put Abraham's story into a perspective you might better relate to. A person has lived in the same house for more than 45 years. Let's say that this person has been married for nearly 50 years and raised four children in this house. This home is the central focal point of lifelong memories. Even the grandchildren and great grandchildren regard their grandparents' home as the most special, sentimental place on earth. Inside the house, the walls are almost totally covered with photographs of family—children, aunts and uncles, cousins, brothers, sisters, the family dog, and so on. Everything that pertains to this family's life and familial development is contained within its walls.

Suddenly one day, this house catches on fire because the wiring had never been updated in its 95 years. An electrical fire started in the walls, and before it was ever noticed, flames rapidly spread, consuming everything in their path. Nothing is spared; everything burns to ashes. All of the mementos, the trinkets, the books, Grandma's knitted quilts, Grandpa's favorite caps, the photos, and the videos, all gone—within the blink of an eye, it seems. Just like that, gone! How quickly do you think this family should be able to move forward after experiencing such a devastating loss? Their very souls were vested in that place—all of their most precious memories were conceived there. What now?

No matter how much they will miss their beloved home, they have no choice but to move forward. There is nothing to go back to. Whatever lies ahead is what these folks must embrace, because they simply have no other option. They will have to accept the fact that their lives have been forever changed.

Now, I realize that this is a dire example, one that I would never wish on anyone, not even my worst enemy. But the point I am trying to make is: *when you have nothing to turn back to, you are more prepared to welcome the idea of moving forward.* It should never have to come to that point—better to go willingly than to be thrust out by unwanted circumstances.

Gotta Move On

When God tells you to go, your response should immediately be that you *have* to go forward because there is really nothing to go back to once God has spoken. It may appear there is something to go back to, but it is really an illusion. Had Abraham not followed the Lord's command, the quality of his life could have quickly deteriorated. Although he had the comfort of his family and pleasing, familiar surroundings, God wanted to move him toward a blessing so great, so unimaginable, that neither he nor anyone in his circle of influence could ever have grasped it.

That is why he had to get away from his kindred, his townspeople—you know, the familiar faces—and go where no one knew him. His people would only be a distraction to the fulfillment of God's plan. God is not opposed to your family's witnessing the greatness that comes as a result of serving Him. However, God knows that there are times when He has to remove you from the people who know you so well, that they can never see you beyond where you are right now. Their limiting mind-sets will inevitably hinder your own view of yourself, short-circuiting your blessing. Remember, a prophet is never accepted in his own hometown.

Some folks cannot bear the fact that you have succeeded and are enjoying the blessings you have right now. Really, it bothers them. It hits them at the very core of their being. It's okay for you to live in a modest house, but definitely not a palatial mansion with servants' quarters. It's fine for you to drive a used Hyundai Sonata but don't roll up in a Bentley Continental Flying Spur! When you do, everyone who knows you, or knew you, they will seek to reduce you to the image that they had in their mind of you.

As sad as it sounds, your family has an image of you that only goes but so far. It's hard to break out of the paradigms that others want to create for your life.

You are very fortunate if you have family members who believe in you so much they *expect* you to soar to the highest altitudes. That, unfortunately, is not the norm. Honestly, most family members don't do it intentionally. They don't seek to reduce you to their image because they are trying to hurt you. The reason why they do it is because they are inwardly afraid of your becoming *more* than they are. When you do that, you expose how they have settled for less in life, without your even trying to do so. So they would rather you just stay the same old way you always were—live the same old place, drive the same old car, wear the same old clothes, and die in the same old spot that they refused to let you move away from. Nobody ever liked pioneers. They tend to shake our comfortable places, make us feel we have just *settled*.

The longer you are associated with and surrounded by people who desire to hold you back or that want to keep the same image of you that they've always had, the more you will begin to acquiesce to their demands. You will allow them to reshape your life into *their* image. You *will* begin to be like the people you hang around and spend time eating and fellowshipping with. That's why it is so important to me to surround myself with people who believe that I can go forward and fulfill the purposes of God in the earth. I don't have time for anyone who doesn't want to go forward, worse yet, who doesn't want to see *me* go forward.

My association with them will inhibit my growth and development. Never minimize the power of influence. You must be careful to surround yourself with people who will encourage you on your journey, not discourage you. My hanging out with them will cause me to become sympathetic toward their lethargic conditions and shallow vision of life. And the longer I wait, the more I become transformed into *their* image, not God's. So I've got to get away even though I don't know where I am going, realizing that as I go forward, I am moving closer to the perfect will of God.

Lot's Wife Went the Wrong Way

And it came to pass, when they had brought them forth abroad, that he said, Escape for thy life; look not behind thee, neither stay thou in all the plain; escape to the mountain, lest thou be consumed. ...But his wife looked back from behind him, and she became a pillar of salt (Genesis 19:17, 26 KJV).

Remember Lot's wife (Luke 17:32).

The Book of Genesis records for us the story of the destruction of the city of Sodom. Preceding this narrative, God had conversed with Abraham concerning the unrighteous standing of the citizens of the city. Abraham prayed and pleaded with God to spare the city if only 10 righteous people could be found in the city. Unfortunately there was no such luck for that city. Can you imagine a city where there was not 10 righteous folk?

Lot was in the wrong place at the wrong time. He should have never been in the city of Sodom. He should have cast his lot with

Abraham and stayed close to him. Like Eve his eyes got him in trouble. He looked at the plains of Jordan where Sodom was located and got distracted. Lot took his family to Sodom while Abraham remained in Canaan.

After Abraham had pleaded with God, the two angels headed to Sodom. You remember the story. After an encounter with the people of Sodom, the two angels told Lot to take his family and leave the city. The city was going down!

Lot got his family together and left the city. Everyone in the family seemed to heed these divine instructions except for one, Lot's beloved wife. For unstated reasons, her curiosity began to drive her crazy. She began reminiscing on her life back in Sodom. She played around with these thoughts so much, she just had to take one small peek to see what she was giving up in order to move forward. As soon as she made that foolish move, she immediately turned into a pillar of salt and became totally worthless to God, to herself, and to her family.

Some scholars have argued that Lot's wife could not give up her sinful tendencies and looked back in curiosity trying to determine if her decision to follow her family to safe ground was a good decision after all. That claim may have some validity to it, but I find it weak. What I personally believe happened here is that Lot's wife looked back because she simply could not believe that what God had in store for her would compare to what she had become accustomed to. This same train of thinking exists today in far too many believers' lives. You cannot reach out to your future if you insist on holding on to your past. That is an incontrovertible principle.

Harold Wilson, one of the most prominent British politicians of the 20th century, once said, "he who rejects change is the architect of decay. The only human institution that rejects progress is the cemetery."[13] God is the author of change, and those who cannot flow with that change will be subject to decay.

God is only trying to release you from your past so that you can become something of much greater value. But as long as you believe that where you are right now is as good as it gets, you'll die a slow death of insignificance. It is the greatest insult to God to infer that He is not capable of providing a better place for you, especially when He is the one requiring you to go to that unfamiliar place. And the same way that God took care of Prophet Elijah, causing ravens to feed him by a brook called Cherith, He will take care of you *if* you will only trust Him.

Obedience Brings the Blessing

If ye be willing and obedient, ye shall eat the good of the land: But if ye refuse and rebel, ye shall be devoured with the sword: for the mouth of the Lord hath spoken it (Isaiah 1:19-20 KJV).

God wants to take you to a place where no one could ever dream you'd go—a place you would laugh at because you would think it was too lofty of an attainment for little ol' you. That's the place where God wants you to go. But you have to recognize that only obedience will get you to that place, nothing less. And obedience always requires you doing something that works opposite to what your flesh desires.

Contingencies—contingencies are usually how God works. I've stated this earlier. If you do this, I'll do that. "If you go wherever I tell you to go, then I'll make sure that it'll be worthwhile. I throw in plenty of extras. But first I want to make sure that you will obey Me no matter what." There are many people who are willing to obey God when all of the elements are conducive to obeying Him. I mean, when we have reasons to obey Him it makes it more convenient and safe than if we just have to take Him at His word without having any other form of collateral. Obey first; inquire after!

Road Maps Not Needed Here

God doesn't play the conditional game, although we think He does. "If you bless me with a whole lot of money first, then I'll pay my tithes. When I get a brand-new car, then I'll come to church. If I land a role in a movie, then I'll bless the church. When God heals me, then I'll serve Him." Sorry to break your religious bubble, but it just doesn't work that way, even though we might like it to. Many believers think that God's orders come with MapQuest road directions. "Lord, I'll go if You give me some directions, but if not I'll just wait until You get it together."

Road maps are for doubters. Great men and women of faith never have maps. They just go and trust that God will safely take them to a place worthy of their travel.

Faith-filled people just know in the core of their being that God will never take them to a place that is not right. If God is the originator of your blessing, you will never be able to digest it at first. It will *always* be larger than you are and no map would ever be able to get you there, since God wants you to go as He instructs.

Patrick Overton, author and educator, put it this way:

When you have come to the edge
Of all light that you know
And are about to drop off into the darkness
Of the unknown,
Faith is knowing
One of two things will happen:
There will be something solid to stand on or
You will be taught to fly.[14]

If you were to have a map, you would never listen for the voice of the Lord. But without a map you will be inclined to follow only His directions, listen only to His instructions, and heed only His voice. Without a map, you have no other method of knowing how to get where you are going other than to listen to Him. The whole idea is that God is determined to get you in a place where you fully rely on Him. And any other voice but His, you'll block out, knowing that additional voices will only bring gross confusion, causing you to travel in endless circles, making no real progress toward His intended goal for you.

How Success Is Defined

Go wherever God says and you will be a success. Do whatever He tells you to do and you will win. Those two simple sentences sum up the entire definition for success. I realize that we live in a society that defines success in a totally different way. In Beverly Hills, success is defined by what you can afford to drive, the size of the house that you live in, the designer wardrobe that you own, and by the type of people that you hang around with. Although none of these things are inherently evil in and of themselves, they are not an accurate depiction of how God views success. The picture that God paints of success is radically different from our definition of success.

God never views success by what you have and what you've merited or even the amount of knowledge that you've gathered over the years. He only measures success by one thing: Have you done what He has said? For example, if God tells you to stand in a corner for a solid year, not to move from that corner, and you successfully do that, He qualifies you a success. You will have to know that if He told you to stand in the corner, then He will surely send you total provision for as long as you remain there. The problem is, we can become so enamored by what other people believe about us that we can miss God.

There are people who are in the pulpit who should not be there. I am not saying that they are not saved and don't really love the Lord, but God just did not tell them to preach. He may have told them to be a lawyer, a doctor, the owner of a child-care facility, a mechanic, or a professor. But the persuasive mind-set of the Church convinced them that what would most please God would be going into the ministry. As a result, they wind up struggling to make ends meet, losing their families, and being altogether ineffective. Why? It was simply because they did not do exactly what God told them to do.

As insane as it may sound, if God told you to close your eyes, wiggle your nose, while standing on one foot, and you completed the silly exercise, you'd have just entered into the halls of godly success. Neither you nor I have the right or authority to qualify God's actions or His appeals. What He asks of us does not *have* to make sense. It does not have to fit within the framework of our experience.

A Testing or a Blessing

In fact, it may be something that we just know we cannot do or have never done before. But if God orders it, He's *already* made the provision long before He asked you to follow Him. It is not that God is trying to test you, as so many believe. Tests are not required since God knows what you are going to do and how you will respond in any given situation.

The reason is not for testing, but for blessing. God wants to bless you big time! But He knows that if you can't follow simple instructions without balking, complaining, and qualifying, then you are not ready for the blessing. You may think you are, but your responsiveness to His word is the acid test that will ultimately prove whether or not you are capable of handling what He is getting ready to dish out. Knowing that your entire attitude needs to change is a major part of the process.

And your speech should be in perfect alignment with your attitude. You ask, "How will I know that my attitude and verbal communication have become one with God's thoughts?" You will know it when you answer His call with the right answers:

Q: "Where are you going?"

A: "I'm going wherever God says to go."

Q: "How are you going to get there?"

A: "I don't really know, but for now, that really doesn't matter, I'm just going to go."

Chapter 4

Many Are Called But Few Are Recruited

So David said to Michal, "It was before the Lord, who chose me above your father and above all his house, to appoint me ruler over the people of the Lord, over Israel; therefore I will celebrate before the Lord (2 Samuel 6:21 NASB).

So the last shall be first, and the first last: for many be called, but few chosen (Matthew 20:16 KJV).

You never choose God—God chooses you. Although in most churches we make an appeal every service for people to accept the Lordship of Jesus Christ, what you see is only the tip of the iceberg. You probably think that these people heard a convicting message, were pricked in their heart and conscience, and in response to the message, they made the choice to get up out of their seats and walk down the aisle to publicly choose God. That has been the commonly accepted premise for many years. But I am here to tell you, there is much more than you will never know that influenced that decision.

Now I am not suggesting that the people who have heard the message are not making a choice to follow Christ of their own free volition. That's not what I am saying. The point that I am trying to make here is that long before they made their choice, God had already made His choice—a choice that ultimately supersedes anyone's choice. Here's the deal. God sets us up for the choices that we make. Everywhere that you have traveled since you were born, each and every person who has crossed your path, every school you attended, the neighborhood that you were reared in, and the parents to whom you were born, were all a part of God's master plan to woo you back to Him.

Who Does the Choosing?

As humans, and especially as Americans, we are used to the power of the choice. We can freely choose where we live, where we work, what we eat, what kind of car we drive, and who our friends will be. But when it comes to God, we must remember that God is not a commodity. He is not something that you can fit in your garage or hang in your closet. God is not something to be cleaned up, filed away, pocketed, or compartmentalized. God does not tidily fit into your worldview. God is not there as part of the furniture, some appendage that I parade before others in order to create a certain image about myself or fall back on to shore up an argument.

You were always *His* choice; you just did not realize it. Once He has decided, He gives you the opportunity to respond. He will allow you to drift away if you chose, and to go through some of the most trying of circumstances, in order to drive you back into His loving arms. He wanted you in an isolated position so that you would recognize that He has been trying to express His overwhelming love for you from the moment you were born. He is the one who set the whole thing up, not you! God gets great glory from knowing that you can laugh at your past hardships when you realize that they are not comparable to what you are experiencing now or are soon going to experience.

Moreover whom He did predestinate, them He also called: and whom He called, them He also justified: and whom He justified, them He also glorified (Romans 8:30 KJV).

He is the One who caused every human messenger and every angel to cross your path over the years. You did not know it then neither did you understand exactly what was happening. It was all preplanned. He is the Divine Intruder! Long before you were born God orchestrated an ingenious way to get you right where He wanted you to be. God did not manipulate or control you or even force you to love Him and serve Him. He only planted seeds all around you that, once fully developed, would give any thinking individual the needed resolve and passion to serve Him wholeheartedly.

Jesus Christ was the ultimate Seed planted into the core of your being influencing you to the right choice about your future. Although Jesus' sacrificial death was a very obvious expression of how much God loved us and to what great lengths He would go in order to persuade us to be with Him, billions of people still miss the very apparent message. Sometimes in life, people have a hard time recognizing the most obtrusive signs. I don't really know why people miss it. Really, I can't explain it.

What I do know is that people are often prone to notice the smaller details rather than the large ones. For example, you can give a woman one freshly picked, sweet-smelling rose, and it may leave a more lasting impression than a whole bouquet. There are times when a lady will take notice of how you stand to honor her or open the car door for her, or allow her to enter through a door first. It's the small things that count a lot. What we consider the bigger things sometimes get lost in the maze of the little things.

That is why God uses the small, outrageous, and vague methods to draw your attention to Him. He approaches us through ordinary and inconspicuous people to bring a little sunshine into your life. He has been known to use your next-door neighbor, grandma, your frat brother, your old high school chum, your old drug partner, or even an old flame in order to communicate the message that you are *chosen* and He wants you now.

He even uses foolish methods like preaching to convey His message to mankind. Now I realize that preaching has gone through a metamorphosis and somehow survived. It has been condemned and thoroughly scrutinized by those who deem it unnecessary and imprudent. But I am here to defend this foolish, often emotional method called preaching.

ROMERO, TERESA RACHE

Check Item Out By:
Sun May 29

05/19/16 11:58AM

I'll be the first to admit that although I don't really understand why preaching, just words, draws people to Him, I just know it does. I'm not completely knowledgeable about how airplanes can stay in the sky, but I know that they do. I don't have to understand all of the laws of aviation and lift in order for flight to work for me. I have to believe because they work. God even says that preaching is a foolish method.

For Christ sent me not to baptize, but to preach the gospel: not with wisdom of words, lest the cross of Christ should be made of none effect. For the preaching of the cross is to them that perish foolishness; but unto us which are saved it is the power of God. For it is written, I will destroy the wisdom of the wise, and will bring to nothing the understanding of the prudent. Where is the wise? where is the scribe? where is the disputer of this world? hath not God made foolish the wisdom of this world? For after that in the wisdom of God the world by wisdom knew not God, it pleased God by the foolishness of preaching to save them that believe. For the Jews require a sign, and the Greeks seek after wisdom: But we preach Christ crucified, unto the Jews a stumblingblock, and unto the Greeks foolishness; but unto them which are called, both Jews and Greeks, Christ the power of God, and the wisdom of God. Because the foolishness of God is wiser than men; and the weakness of God is stronger than men (1 Corinthians 1:17-25 KJV).

The passion of Paul, written in these verses, declares that the foolishness of God is always far greater and more effective than the collective knowledge of intellectual men. It is foolishness to them that perish. The two groups of people that are targeted by Paul are the society of unbelievers and skeptics, and obedient, faithful believers. Those people in the first category believe that preaching in the name of the Lord Jesus is idiocy.

The latter group believes that this same gospel publicly spoken by anointed people will be translated into the power of God. For them it is divinely effective in its ability to deliver them from the power of guilt, shame, and pollution of sin. God called both groups to be reconciled to the Father, yet He chose you. Just knowing that truth should give you every reason to not only feel honored, but to also look forward to the rewards that comes with this selection and your response.

The Privilege of Being Selected

Blessed are they which are persecuted for righteousness' sake: for theirs is the kingdom of heaven (Matthew 5:10 KJV).

There are times when you may feel as if the things that you've gone through in life, even after salvation, are so great they will forfeit God's choice of you. You may feel that you are going through trying circumstances for the sake of Christ and His Kingdom and things are not panning out the way you thought they would. After enduring a particular kind of struggle for years, you begin to wonder whether being selected by God was really that great a deal after all. Is the sorrow of this present time worth the eventual goal?

A 19th-century poet wrote, "Trials, temptations, disappointments—all these are helps instead of hindrances, if one uses them rightly. They not only test the fiber of character but strengthen it. Every conquering temptation represents a new fund of moral energy."[15] The beauty of a trial is in the eye of the beholder. We can look at a trial and think that God does not love us and that we do not have the strength to stand. Or, we can observe God's love in the trial and discover His grace in the midst of the trial.

I am here to tell you that the end of your journey will be worth everything that you may go through along the way. The prize is worth the struggle that you are going through right now. It is always a privilege to be selected by God, no matter what your circumstances may tell you. Honestly, I have to admit that you do not always feel the greatest *while* you are going through the process that will take you to your expected end. Sometimes the pain is so intense, you cannot see the next step in front of you. That is when you must hold on to the promise that what you are dealing with will not last forever, and when you come *through* it, you are going to come out on top.

I like what Helen Keller wrote about the value of a trial. She certainly had her share of pain and heartache. Here is what she said: "Character cannot be developed in ease and quiet. Only through experiences of trial and suffering can the soul be strengthened, vision cleared, ambition inspired, and success achieved."[16]

The Glory of Being Chosen

Do you think that Queen Esther considered herself a privileged person to be selected by God to speak on the behalf of her

Jewish people, knowing that she could lose her life in the process? I believe she did. She understood that if she could pass through these deep waters and survive, she would forever change the destiny of a people.

To be selected to be a Secret Service agent, protecting the life of the President of the United States of America, is a great honor. These men and women willingly put their lives in grave peril day after day to defend the person and the legacy of our presidents. You may think, "I'd never do that. It just isn't worth it." Well, you have to have a deep awareness of the value of your calling if you are going to be able to survive the process of bringing you into that calling.

Any persons who are going to be within arm's length of the President are, of necessity, going to have to undergo a thorough winnowing process. Their lives will be under a microscope, as it were. An in-depth background check will be run on not just them, but their family members as well. Any close relative in their life who has some kind of black mark on their record could negatively impact the would-be agent. A prospective Secret Service agent must of course be extremely fit, both physically and mentally. They must have achieved academic heights. Even the way they stand and present themselves is important. Their posture and poise is factored into the decision-making process. And *loyalty* is key! It is in this area that the authorities will do the most probing and investigation.

They want to make sure that if and when the President should come under fire, that agent would not hesitate to give up his life to save his charge. Loyalty would not be an issue to him or her. Still, only a few people are going to be chosen for the job out of many applicants. And those persons can be justifiably proud to have been not only considered for the job, but *chosen*.

In the same way, you should feel honored that God chose you. He could have chosen so many others, but He chose *you*. There is a glory attached to being chosen by God.

You may look at your life and wonder why He would choose someone who has such obvious flaws and imperfections? The cool thing is that God has this habit of looking beyond the outward frame and seeing into our hearts. He sees what others do not see. The Lord knows what is in my heart, what is in your heart, and that is why He has chosen us. In fact, Paul noticed this same quality about the God that he served. Paul told the Corinthians that God chooses the weak and foolish of this world to work out His purposes. Why? It's a *glory* thing! God often passes over the strong because anything they accomplish can be attributed to their strength. But when a weak person accomplishes what should be impossible for them, people recognize that God has empowered them, and He is glorified.

Why Did He Choose You?

Even every one that is called by My name: for I have created him for My glory, I have formed him; yea, I have made him (Isaiah 43:7 KJV).

You were created to bring glory to God. Virtually everything that you accomplish in life should give glory to God. When you go through the fire and come out without the scent of smoke,

God gets the glory. After suffering with cancer and having chemotherapy treatments for more than a year, only to discover that you've been completely healed in the process by Christ the Healer, God is glorified. And God takes great delight in choosing unassuming people, those whom others would pass right over, to go through the grueling efforts to become approved for the blessing. *Weakness is a great backdrop for the glory of God!*

A Man Called Job

Job was just this kind of humble and inconspicuous person. *"There was a man in the land of Uz, whose name was Job; and that man was perfect and upright, and one that feared God, and eschewed evil"* (Job 1:1 KJV). Job obviously passed the character test with God since he was labeled as a perfect and upright man, a compliment that is rarely received. Everything appeared to be going well in Job's life. He had ten children—seven sons and three daughters. He was a business owner with great possessions. *"His substance also was seven thousand sheep, and three thousand camels, and five hundred yoke of oxen, and five hundred she asses, and a very great household; so that this man was the greatest of all the men of the east"* (Job 1:3 KJV).

Each of the livestock that he owned represented a particular business that we would have an equivalent to in our modern society. Job owned 7,000 sheep. Sheep provide wool. Wool makes clothing. Hence Job was in the *textile industry*. Next, he owned 500 yoke of oxen (that is 1,000 oxen). What was the primary purpose of oxen in that agrarian society? Oxen were used to till the ground, preparing it for the planting of crops. So Job owned a *produce business*.

I'm not finished yet. He also owned 500 female asses. Mules were used as beasts of burden to carry heavy loads. So today's equivalent would be a *trucking business*. Finally, we're told Job owned 3,000 camels. Camels were known for carrying lighter loads and small packages. So it is safe to suggest that Mr. Job also owned and operated a *FedEx franchise*.

He lived in a beautiful mansion, and some of his children owned their own homes as well. So by all standards, both then and now, we can establish that Job was an extremely successful man. Because of this respected position in his community, his obvious love for family, and his passion for commerce we can understand why the Scriptures say that *"this man was the greatest of all the men of the east."* It seemed as if Job led a charmed life. But someone else was watching him who thought things were going a little too well for Job. And when things are going well in your life, satan gets angry.

Now there was a day when the sons of God came to present themselves before the Lord, and satan came also among them. And the Lord said unto satan, Whence comest thou? Then satan answered the Lord, and said, From going to and fro in the earth, and from walking up and down in it. And the Lord said unto satan, Hast thou considered My servant Job, that there is none like him in the earth, a perfect and an upright man, one that feareth God, and escheweth evil? Then satan answered the Lord, and said, Doth Job fear God for nought? Hast not Thou made an hedge about him, and about his house, and about all that he hath on every side? Thou hast blessed the work of his hands, and his substance is increased in the land. But put

*forth Thine hand now, and touch all that he hath, and he
will curse Thee to Thy face* (Job 1:6-11 KJV).

The devil cannot stand to see God's people prospering. So he
just has to stick his big nose into Job's business. Off he goes to con-
front God on this issue. Actually, it almost appears in this story
that God dangles Job in front of satan, taunting him. This tells me
He was so sure of His servant that He almost challenges satan to
test one of His best. Understand that when God selects you for
your destiny, He already knows that you have what it takes to survive whatever suffering it takes to attain it. God knew that Job
would stay the course, no matter what he lost. Satan, in his finite-
ness, thought the only reason Job served God was for the *stuff*—
the material possessions. He dared God to take everything away
from Job, all of His earthly possessions, and see how long he
would last. Why, "*he will curse Thee to Thy face.*" God took the
dare and all hell broke loose...

Before he knew what hit him, every conceivable (and incon-
ceivable) thing that could have happened to Job, did happen to
him. He lost all of his businesses. His children were all killed while
partying in their oldest brother's home. His wife grew angry with
him and abandoned the faith, encouraging him to do the same.
Then Job contracted a fleshing-eating disease causing his flesh to
produce puss-filled boils. Talk about Murphy's Law! Then to add
insult to injury, his friends, Eliphaz the Temanite, Bildad the
Shuhite, and Zophar the Naamathite (see Job 2:11) came to visit
him to offer him their invaluable advice. "Basically, Job, it's all
your fault! You must have done something to deserve this!" With
friends like that, who needs enemies?

Job finally became so overwhelmed and depressed with the whole situation that he began to wish he had never been born. *"After this opened Job his mouth, and cursed his day. And Job spake, and said, Let the day perish wherein I was born, and the night in which it was said, There is a man child conceived"* (Job 3:1-3 KJV). An entire book on the Old Testament was devoted to this man's story—the Book of Job. It is an ancient book chronicling the details of a simple man's struggle and eventual victory. If you haven't read it lately, you just might want to pick it up. I have a feeling that it will make your circumstances pale in comparison. Job finally reached the point where he, too, like you, began to wonder why God chose him to travel down this intense grief-stricken road. Worse yet, it appeared that he was forced to travel this road alone. Where was God? I *know* that you have asked that question.

By now you've probably pulled out the box of tissues to wipe away the tears prompted by this awful, depressing story. This is a very sad story, but it not the end of the story. Believe me, I might join you in your weeping were it not for one thing: The story doesn't end there. Throughout the remaining chapters of the book, Job experiences a number of character-building moments through which he learns the most valuable lessons of his entire life. In the end, Job gets to laugh, because in the end, God restores everything back to him, with even more heaped on top.

So the Lord blessed the latter end of Job more than his beginning: for he had fourteen thousand sheep, and six thousand camels, and a thousand yoke of oxen, and a thousand she asses. He had also seven sons and three daughters. And he called the name of the first, Jemima; and the name of the second, Kezia; and the name of the third, Keren-hap-puch. And in all the land were no women found so fair as the daughters of Job: and their father gave them inheritance among their brethren. After this lived Job an hundred and forty years, and saw his sons, and his sons' sons, even four generations. So Job died, being old and full of days (Job 42:12-17 KJV).

Job got *double for his trouble.* It is interesting to note that Job's name in the Hebrew is *Iyowb* and its literal meaning is "hated or persecuted." When God has an affinity for you, you will always be hated and persecuted by the forces of evil. But don't be discouraged—you're in good company. They hated the prophets; they hated Jesus. They victimized John Wesley and Jonathan Edwards, and they persecuted Bishop Noel Jones. Job was hated, and you are too. The bottom line is that it really doesn't matter how *they* feel as long as *you* know that *God's got your back.* In the final analysis you are going to get through with far more than you could even dream of. It's worth it, my friend! This is the picture that you must keep before you as you walk through the valley of affliction and sorrow.

The Garden of Gethsemane—God's College

And I said unto him, Sir, thou knowest. And he said to me, These are they which came out of great tribulation, and have washed their robes, and made them white in the blood of the Lamb (Revelation 7:14 KJV).

Why did you have to go through all the things you have gone through in your life? Is there any meaning to your sorrow? There is a divine purpose to your suffering and trials. Just as diamonds are formed under the most extreme pressure, *all* that you have endured has made you who you are and what you are. You were made into something more valuable than you could begin to imagine. If you wanted to earn a college degree, you'd have to go through four years of concentrated, rigorous study under the most trying circumstances. You'd have to go to classes at least two to three times each week. Most professors suggest that you study two hours per each hour of class to get the best possible return on your investment. Midterms, finals, term papers, essays, and tests are all a part of the process of making you a man or woman of the letter, a degreed individual. Anything worth having in life will always cost you something. Nothing is going to come to you on a silver platter served up by angelic hosts.

Suppose you drop out for a semester, or take a year off to work in order to earn some money. You will only delay the process. You can do two years and take two years off but that doesn't mean that you are going to be able to graduate with those who stuck it out. You have to endure the process until it is over. You may not always want to go through it, but go through it you must. It is the only doorway that will lead you into God's plans and purposes for your life. Any shortcuts will only lead to darker places and delay the fulfillment of God's dream for your life.

Then saith He unto them, My soul is exceeding sorrowful, even unto death: tarry ye here, and watch with Me. And He went a little further, and fell on His face, and prayed, saying, O My Father, if it be possible, let this cup pass from Me:

nevertheless not as I will, but as Thou wilt (Matthew 26:38-39 KJV).

Jesus had to drink the cup. There was no other way. At Gethsemane, Jesus had His own moment of weakness as He contemplated the pain He would have to endure. Even though He knew that it would be worth it all, He still had a "moment." It was an anxious moment. It was a fear-ridden moment. It was a contemplative moment as He counted the cost.

Have you ever had a "moment?" Let me define a "moment." It is the time when you are suspended between the reality of life as you know it, and life as it could be if you obey God. You know what you need to do, and you know God told you to do it, but for just a "moment" you pause to consider the cost.

You know there is no other way, but you still, just for a "moment," wonder what things would be like if you did not have to go through this. Jesus had a "moment," wondering how He would be able to hang suspended between man's world and God's world. How would He be able to endure being disconnected from God, His Father? It was only a moment—but it probably seemed like an eternity to Him that night in the garden. I imagine that He came to the conclusion that He could bear up under anything that man in his ignorance and fear might do to Him, but the thought of being separated from His Father for even a brief time was almost more than He could bear. That's when He cried out, "*O My Father, if it be possible, let this cup pass from Me.*"

But then, without waiting for a response, our Savior bowed His head and whispered, "*Nevertheless not as I will, but as Thou wilt.*" God, it's not about Me, but about Your will, Your plan. It's

Your Kingdom, and it's Your Glory. When you get a clear vision into the invisible realm, you will be given strength to endure the fear and the pain of your trials. You may not *want* to go through, but you've *got* to. God chose you for this assignment, and He's not going to let you off until He brings you into every single thing He promised you. Though the promise seems to delay, always remember, He is faithful and will give you great grace—the power to deliver you into your destiny.

T.S. Elliot, in his classic poem *The Hollow Men* drafted these searching words:

Between the idea
And the reality
Between the motion
And the act
Falls the Shadow

Between the conception
And the creation
Between the emotion
And the response
Falls the Shadow.[17]

Between the choice that God made for your life and the fulfillment of that choice there is the shadow. There is the shadow of what you have to walk through to reach the fulfillment of God's ultimate idea for your life. The shadow will only pass when you decide to let go of your choices and follow His choice for your life.

Chapter 5

God—
Never Recognized,
Always Revealed

God is never recognized; He is always revealed. The anointing is revealed. That is expressly why some people have such a difficult time discerning whether the power of God is actually upon someone. In many instances in Scripture, Jesus was anointed to heal the sick, raise the dead, and perform miracles. Often the Pharisees would accuse Him of being empowered by the devil to be able to perform these miraculous acts of benevolence.

There were times when Jesus would openly declare who He was, what His purpose on earth was, and His thoughts concerning His death, burial, and resurrection. Because of His esoteric nature people wrote Him off as some nutcase on an ego trip and would often attribute His works as being of the devil. *"And many of them said, He hath a devil, and is mad; why hear ye Him? Others said, These are not the words of Him that hath a devil. Can a devil open the eyes of the blind?"* (John 10:20-21 KJV). As we can see in this verse, people who listened to and observed Jesus came down on opposing sides. One group accused Jesus of being a demon-possessed lunatic. The other group was made up of spiritually aware people who began to ask questions concerning His healing powers, realizing that the devil would not empower anyone to heal sick people.

Despite the numerous miracles that Jesus performed right in front of the eyes of the crowds, they continued to dispute their validity. The Pharisees refused to acknowledge Jesus as an anointed vessel, one who had supernatural powers to effect change in the earth realm. Despite their gross denial about Jesus' obvious spiritual giftings, Jesus was still who He was. Trying to prove He was God would have been fruitless because they would never have seen it no matter how hard they tried. Some things cannot be seen, until first the Father has revealed them. The Scripture below chronicles and validates this same concept.

In Matthew 16, Jesus posed a very interesting question to His disciples. "Who do men say that I am?" That question caused them to resurrect from their memory the different responses they had heard from both the religious people and the common folk. As intriguing as that question is, the next question was the critical one: "Who do *you* say I am?" The reason why it was not a very weighty question was that Jesus' greatest concern was their personal answer to that question. Although the Pharisees continually provoked and taunted Jesus trying to discredit His ministry, they could not succeed, primarily because they were not within

His *inner circle*. Jesus was concerned whether or not the light of revelation had dawned in their spirit.

Considering Those in the Inner Circle

Understand that it is not who is outside your circle that matters most, but rather those who are in your inner circle. Those who are in your outer circle, though you are familiar with them, do not have the intimacy to be able to influence you like those who are right at the core of your day-to-day activities. You can be eating at a restaurant, and the restaurant is completely filled with customers. You may recognize the face of certain people or may even know some of the customers personally. But the only ones who should really matter to you are the people eating with you, the ones in close range.

The people who eat at your table and dine out with you regularly are the ones whom you should consider your intimate connections. You don't break bread with just anybody, only the special ones. So when Jesus asked His disciples, "Who do men say that I am?" He was working from the outside inward. The disciples who responded to His inquiry revealed, in that moment, something about themselves that was otherwise hidden. They revealed that they were not as close to Jesus as they thought they were.

Anais Nin, a French novelist, described the power of the inner circle in this way. "Each friend represents a world in us, a world possibly not born until they arrive, and it is only by this meeting that a new world is born."[18] Jesus was that friend. There was an undiscovered world within each one of Jesus' disciples that would not be born until He came into their life. Revelation was waiting for His appearing into the lives of these men.

When people do not know who you really are, it shows that they are not as close to you as they believe they are. Or, if not that, it could be that they are not very close to God—because great people are never known by the flesh. They are known by the spirit. God has to reveal it to them. So the disciples, the ones following Jesus from afar, responded by saying that some were saying Jesus was Elijah the Prophet resurfaced, others that He was John the Baptist reincarnated, while others thought He was Jeremiah the Prophet.

Getting the Question Right

What the disciples did not know is that all of the answers, although correct in part, were wrong when it came to the heart of the question. It was true that people saw Jesus in light of His ancestral spiritual lineage, but that was not really who Jesus was. Who cares what outsiders think of you? What matters most is what the insiders believe about you. You may have great influence as a pastor/evangelist. Everywhere you preach as an evangelist, you should have a favorable response from the people to whom you minister. However, they do not really *know* you. They can't come close. They can only know what you are *known for*. They won't be able to tell people who you really are. At best they can show great appreciation for you.

But the people who can begin to answer that question, "Who do men say that I am?" will be the ones that I preach to every week. They are with me, and they have more of an ability to access my value to them. You cannot truly know another person based on one scenario, one setting. You need to be around them in many different settings. I've often said, "If I can preach a great message at home, then I can preach that message successfully anywhere in the world." Why is that? Because that message has passed the test on the proving ground of familiar soil, which is the most difficult soil to produce anything in. Who you are in the private will be reflected in what you do in the public place.

Peter's Right Answer

I believe that Jesus must have felt frustration that none of the disciples could answer that question correctly. His disciples were so focused on others' opinions that they could not even recognize the significance of the question, *"Whom do men say that I the Son of man am?"* Each disciple should be able to answer this question based upon his own personal experience with Christ. Only one disciple got it!

Peter spoke up, "I know the answer! You are the Christ, the Son of the Living God." *"And Jesus answered and said unto him, Blessed art thou, Simon Barjona: for flesh and blood hath not revealed it unto thee, but My Father which is in Heaven."* Peter did not answer out of his daily experience of walking, talking, and eating with the man Jesus. Even though Jesus asked His disciples about the son of man, Peter recognized that Jesus was more than just a man. He was flesh but He was also God. Peter looked beyond the flesh and truly saw that this Man for whom he had left everything was, indeed, from a different realm.

Jesus knew intuitively that Peter was not able to answer that question because of a learned background in Messianic teachings. In truth, Peter was one of the unlearned, under-educated disciples, a simple fisherman. No, Jesus knew that something else had to have given Peter this revelation. He knew that God had revealed His true identity to Peter. You can't see who Jesus is. You just have to *know* who He is by the Spirit. If the Spirit doesn't reveal it to you, then you cannot *know*, because God is never recognized, but revealed. You can't get this revelation through school or from books. This revelation comes from a higher source—a much higher source. It is revealed to your spirit by the Spirit. It is important that your spirit remain clean so that it can come to you.

Thou Shalt Be Revealed

If God is never recognized but always revealed, could it be possible that the God inside of you has yet to be revealed? Like Jesus, you at times get frustrated with people when they don't recognize the life of God in you. Don't get mad at them. They can't help it. They can't recognize the God in you because the anointing is invisible. In time, God will reveal it to them.

I am the same person, for all intents and purposes, that I was some 30 years ago. Why is it that people receive me now with open arms when in my twenties they overlooked me? Did I have less of an anointing? Was God not in my life then? I don't believe it was either of those things. The reason they could not see then what people see now is because it had not yet been revealed. God has a place and time when He reveals His masterpieces to the world. Regardless of how much you would like Him to reveal you right away, it just won't happen. Timing is everything, and the timing of your public expression is left in Father's hands.

If He revealed you too soon, there would be repercussions that would follow. Here is an important lesson. *Your character must be equal to your gifting.* So don't get mad and upset when people don't realize your anointing. Don't get all bent out of shape because this sister or that brother doesn't see you as great. They are looking through natural eyes, the realm of the five senses. They can't look past where you are right now. They're looking at the junker that you're driving now because they can't see the car that you're getting ready to drive. They're looking at the subsidized housing that you are living in now, but cannot see the mansion that you are getting ready to move into. And that's perfectly fine. Your day will come!

Besides, some things are not for everybody to know anyhow. But as sure as God is God, "*Thou shalt be revealed.*" You haven't been in this narrow place all these years faithfully serving God, for nothing. You've fought and fought until you could not fight anymore. Because you committed to live by a godly standard, people laughed at you. They said, "Look at her paying her tithes and offering to the church, and she doesn't even have a car or a decent place to live. Ha! Ha! Ha!" Don't respond. It's not your time yet. The laughing will stop when you are unveiled as God's beloved.

God's working on some things for you right now, even as you are reading these words. You are getting ready to be revealed. You've been kept a secret long enough. The same people who knew you *in the natural* in the past, will now look at you and see you for what you have always been. Be revealed in Jesus' name!

Hidden But Not Lost

I read an article in the *San Francisco Chronicle* that I thought would crystallize the point that I've been making. The title of the article was "Centuries-Old Murals Revealed in Mission: Dolores Indians' Hidden Paintings Open Window Into S.F.'s Sacred Past." The article was about an amazing discovery by an artist and an archaeologist who both discovered religious mural paintings by the American Indians that are more than 200 years old. The article opens up detailing their finds:

> Two young men, one an artist, the other an archaeologist, crawled over the ancient redwood beams of San Francisco's Mission Dolores earlier this month, opened a trap door, lowered an electric light into a space behind the main altar—and stared into the 18th century.
>
> There, in a space thick with the dust of centuries and dark as a tomb, is a wall of nearly forgotten religious murals, painted in red, black and yellow by Native Americans in 1791 and hidden from public view for 208 years.
>
> The two—freelance artist Ben Wood, 23, and Presidio of San Francisco archaeologist Eric Blind, 29—have rediscovered the old murals, have taken digital photographs of them, and are projecting the images on the inside of the dome of the modern Mission Dolores Basilica next door for all to see.

The murals were never really lost. They were always there, like a forgotten treasure. Information about them surfaced from time to time, most notably in the 1980s, when historian Norman Neuerburg made his way up the wooden spiral staircase to the choir loft, climbed a ladder into the attic, crossed over the interior roof of the mission to the trap door, and lowered himself on a rope ladder to see the murals. He had black-and-white sketches made.[19]

I've pulled these few paragraphs from the rest of the article since these make the point that I wish to convey to you. Note that these paintings were kept from the public eye for 208 years and only in the past year have they been rescued from their hiding place. The article says something I thought rather interesting: "The murals were never really lost. They were always there, like a forgotten treasure." You are that forgotten treasure. You might be thinking that you are *lost* and that nobody knows who or where you are. But, listen to me, God knows! You are not lost, and some-day you will be taken out of *hiding*.

Just because everyone does not see you now, does not mean that you have no value. The price tag God has placed upon you is beyond belief. You are all that God purposed in eternity that you would be. You were always there, like a forgotten treasure. The only difference between you and the murals is that you have not been *discovered* yet. God has not forgotten you. He has always had His eye on you. In fact, you are the apple of His eye, and in His time He will proudly reveal you to the world.

There shall not any man be able to stand before thee all the days of thy life: as I was with Moses, so I will be with thee: I will not fail thee, nor forsake thee (Joshua 1:5 KJV).

Chapter 6

He Who Laughs Last

If past history was all there was to the game, the richest people would be librarians.[20]

—Warren Buffett

In Chapter 2, I pointed out the danger of being too quick to laugh, as when Abraham laughed at God's Word to him about fathering a son in his old age. You want to laugh in the end when the promise has been fulfilled, not the beginning with a laugh of unbelief. The one to begin the *laughter ceremony* will generally be the most difficult to persuade that the Word of the Lord will actually come to pass. The first "laughers" are those who will throw up everything in their past and present as ammunition to prove that they simply do not qualify for the blessings of God. This is the laugh of doubt, derision, and disdain. Also the first laughers generally allow the people in their lives to compound their problem of unbelief by constantly pointing to the unfulfilled dreams of their past. Whenever you navigate the waters of past disappointment, you will drown in disbelief.

In sales, there is a commonly held belief that after a presentation has been made for a particular product (could be a car, a Kirby vacuum cleaner, television set, home improvement goods, etc....) and the offer has been put on the table, the first to speak, loses. Usually after a good salesperson has made his or her sales pitch, the salesperson will present the contract and ask the potential client to sign on the dotted line. The salesperson gently pushes the contract and a pen across the table to the customer and then waits quietly.

If the salesperson is the first to speak, they know they've probably lost the sale. But if the customer speaks first, even if it is for clarification or rebutting the price, the salesperson smiles inwardly. The customer's very act of asking means that deep down, he or she wants to buy the product. They just need a bit more convincing, some type of encouragement that they are making the best choice. If the salesperson speaks prematurely, it means that he has not done an effective job of presenting their product. As a result, the customer is left feeling uncertain, that maybe they are dealing with a novice. So they get up with a, "Well, I'm really not interested."

God Has Made Us to Laugh

Why the sales training lesson? It works very much the same when it comes to the "he who laughs last" versus the "he who laughs first" philosophy. Typically, he who derisively laughs first is the person who really does not believe that he will ever amount to anything. He does not believe he will ever rise above his present situation and become everything God intended him to become. It is within this context of unbelief that when you start revealing your visions and your dreams of a better and brighter future to others that you suddenly find yourself becoming a comedic attraction.

They laugh derisively because they have eyes to see, yet cannot see. They laugh disdainfully because they have ears to hear, yet cannot hear what the Spirit is saying. They have a mouth to speak, but they use it to wield a sword of negativity against you, trying to discourage you from God's plan for your life. But we have a wonderful God who can transform their derisive laughter into laughter of embarrassment when He brings to pass His incredible promise for your life. Truly, the one who laughs last, laughs best! The scene quickly changes from sarcasm to surprise, as they find themselves laughing because they cannot believe you actually held on for so long to what they thought was simply wishful thinking rather than a word from the Lord.

Remember, Abraham and Sarah waited 25 years before Sarah made the statement: "God has made me to laugh." Isaac's very name means laughter. It does not matter how people are laughing—whether from derision or embarrassment—it's your last laugh that will be the sweetest when the fulfillment of your promise arrives. Your laughter will always be shared by you, the God of your promise, and everyone who believed with you.

Everything in life is connected to the proper timing. It's time to laugh when you initially receive the incredible word of promise that you are going to be better than ever. But trust me when I tell you that you will not much feel like laughing as time passes because there is nothing humorous about the process. You will certainly not feel like laughing when everyone you thought was close to you begins to scorn, discredit, and make fun of you. You must understand that the devil always seeks opportunities to humiliate God's people any way he can.

> *And I heard a loud voice saying in heaven, Now is come salvation, and strength, and the Kingdom of our God, and the power of His Christ: for the accuser of our brethren is cast down, which accused them before our God day and night* (Revelation 12:10 KJV).

Don't Believe the Lie

In addition to satan's threefold job description of stealing, killing, and causing destruction, he is also the accuser of the brethren. Part of his daily job is to continuously bring accusations against you to God in hopes that God will cast you away for having missed the mark. According to Scripture, he brings these accusations to God each morning and each evening. The good thing is that every time he does this God continually reminds satan that you are covered by the blood of Jesus. You are forgiven everything—past, present, and future!

Satan does not do this actually believing he can convince God that you are not worth His blessings. He knows all too well how God feels about you, and that He cannot break His promise to His children. What the devil really wants to do is recruit you to become your *own* enemy. He seeks to do this by not only accusing you to God, but by accusing God to you. Sound familiar?

Understand, you are not consciously aware when he is accusing you before God, just as Job had no clue what was transpiring in Heaven—when the Sons of God came to present themselves before the Lord, with satan in their midst. It is distressing to accept that man does not love God, but it is absolutely devastating to accept the lie that God does not love man. Satan wants you to believe you are not worthy and therefore will never live long enough to see the extraordinary promises of God come true in your life. Your consistent faith in God is the only thing that will keep you from succumbing to the wiles of the devil, and ensure that you will laugh last. He, who laughs last, lives and wins.

My Past Is Past

I want to forewarn you that people will be assigned by the devil to distract you and depress you by throwing your past in your face every chance they get. They will almost convince you that because you have a less than a spotless past, God will hold that against you and that you have forfeited your promise. Nothing could be farther from the truth. Never forget that a true friend is someone who understands your past, believes in your future, and accepts you just the way you are.

Contrary to what a lot of Christians believe, when God chose to bless you, He chose to do it before the foundation of the world. His omniscience ensures that our God receives no new information. He has total knowledge of the future and the past. He intimately knew your imperfections *before* He gave you the promise.

If they were able to disqualify you, He would never have promised it in the first place.

God is not holding you hostage for the crazy things that you did when your understanding was not as developed as it is now. He is a loving and forgiving God. He cannot help Himself! Even Abraham, who is called the father of our faith, made a horrible mistake after God gave him His promise of an heir. Like so many believers, Abraham grew tired of waiting for the fulfillment and thought maybe God needed a little help. He just could not see how God could possibly give him a son in his old age with an unenthusiastic, aging wife. He couldn't rest in the promise, so he took matters into his own hands.

At his wife's encouragement, he went ahead and made the decision to sleep with her young maidservant, Hagar. Now we have good news and bad news! Hagar did conceive and Abraham got a son, Ishmael, but it was not the son of promise. Hagar, whose name literally means "flight or emigrant," after some years was sent away from the camp by her mistress, whose wishes she had accommodated. She and her son became a source of shame to Sarah until Sarah finally demanded that Abraham send them away. God was neither contemptuous nor angry with this situation; after all, He saw it coming way down the road. But He was disappointed by Abraham's failure to trust Him against all apparent odds.

Nonetheless, Abraham did not blow his chances. He did not disqualify himself by his fleshly and foolish attempt to *help* God. If Abraham had started to wallow in a sea of pity because of his own shortsightedness, he would have held himself hostage to his mistakes and short-circuited his destiny. Okay, you messed up;

but that does not mean that God won't bless you. Repent and move on. Don't compound your mistake by dwelling on it. Let your past remain in the past. Stop bringing your past into your present, because when you do, you systematically dismantle your future bit by bit.

The apostle Paul was a prime candidate for wallowing in his past misguided efforts to help God. Prior to his God encounter on the Damascus Road, Paul was a notorious threat to the people of the Way, now known as Christians. He was on a holy mission to wipe out this heretical new sect of followers of that itinerant, upstart-preacher named Jesus.

After having his divine encounter, Paul became a believer and immediately began to proselytize everyone he came into contact with. His heart's desire was that everyone would know this Jesus and experience the grace he was so wondrously given. The problem was that people didn't trust him. He had just been killing anyone who confessed a belief in Jesus, and now he was trying to convert people to Him! If anyone had an excuse to dwell on his past, it was Paul.

If he had allowed himself to think long about the people he had tortured and tormented and the innocent lives that he was instrumental in killing, he would have never become one of the greatest apostles in the Church of the Lord Jesus Christ. But he, by the grace of God, came to the point where he had to just put the past behind him once and for all. He accepted, with great sorrow, the fact that there was nothing that he could do to change his past. However, there was plenty that could be done to positively impact his future. To that end, he decided to draft a resolution that would eventually become his creed for life.

Paul's Resolution

Brethren, I count not myself to have apprehended: but this one thing I do, forgetting those things which are behind, and reaching forth unto those things which are before, I press toward the mark for the prize of the high calling of God in Christ Jesus (Philippians 3:13-14 KJV).

Paul narrowed his focus down to one thing, *"forgetting those things which are behind."* God's gonna make you laugh, but He won't do it as long as you are wading in the muddy waters of past failures, past mistakes, or even past victories. The bottom line is: They are all in the past. Never hold yourself, nor allow anyone else to hold you, hostage to your shameful past. If you do, they'll manipulate you and control you for the rest of your life. And someone else will wind up enjoying the life that God predestined for you to live. Move on!

My Crying Days Are Over

And God shall wipe away all tears from their eyes; and there shall be no more death, neither sorrow, nor crying, neither shall there be any more pain: for the former things are passed away (Revelation 21:4 KJV).

Depending on your viewpoint, crying could be looked at as the opposite of laughter, just as joy is to sorrow and grief. Crying then is an outward expression of an inward belief system by which you operate. Consider this: A mother accompanies her son to a court hearing that will decide his fate, whether or not he will go to prison for a crime he has been accused of. If she begins crying even before the judge gives his decision, she is acting under the assumption that her child is going to go to prison. Her tears are indicative of her sorrow and pain over something that has not yet occurred. Her crying and spirit of sorrow have made the possibility, her *reality*. Had she been able to smile and be at peace, a confusing message would have been conveyed to the enemy, that she knew something that he did not. There is a time to cry. But it's not now.

You have got to declare that your crying days are over. In making such a declaration, you are saying that you will no longer give assent, whether mentally or spiritually, to any doubts of God's ability to bring His word to pass.

If you only knew how phenomenal your future was, you'd never give in to tears again. Sorrowful crying is a telltale sign that you really don't believe God's promises to you. You may be staring at an eviction notice, but if God says that you are wealthy then stop crying at the possibility of having nowhere to live. Your crying will only get you that much closer to living on the streets. You'd better start rejoicing because you have to know that God has somehow already worked things out for you.

How God does it should not be important at all. The very fact that He said it should give you enough confidence to believe Him no matter how tough things may get. Why are crying? Deep down inside, do you really believe that it's over, and that you have lost the war? For you, life is just beginning. Your glory days are on the horizon. No need to cry, sisters and brothers. This is only the first act of the *new you*. Sit back and enjoy the show. By the way, the last show was a drama. This one is *Gonna Make You Laugh!*

Now It's Time to Laugh

Sarah quickly got the message that she had insulted God by laughing at His word. She could not see beyond her withered, post-menopausal body and her husband's aged, sagging frame to see what God saw for them. And, by the way, this is most people's problem. Most of us think way too small. You believe that you've arrived at your dreams in life when you get your dream car, your dream home, your dream vacation, your dream job, and your dream connection. The problem is that your dream is too shallow. Goethe once said that we should dream no small dreams for they have no power to move the hearts of men.

What God has planned for you is what you should naturally gravitate toward. Unfortunately, we may have to travel a distance in order to reach a point where God can actually promise us something great that we can believe it. Sarah originally did not believe that God could use her old body to bear a child in her advanced years. She, like too many of us, projected her limitations onto God, making Him into her image. Can God not do what He wants? Can He not do what He says? God is not a man that He should lie. If He gives a word, He will bring it to fruition. Let's read the passage of Scripture below and take careful note how Sarah insulted God without even realizing it.

And they said unto him, Where is Sarah thy wife? And he said, Behold, in the tent. And he said, I will certainly return

*unto thee according to the time of life; and, lo, **Sarah thy
wife shall have a son**. And **Sarah heard it** in the tent door,
which was behind him. Now **Abraham and Sarah were
old** and well stricken in age; and **it ceased to be with Sarah**
after the manner of women. Therefore **Sarah laughed** within herself, saying, After I am waxed old **shall I have pleasure,** my lord being old also? And the Lord said unto
Abraham, **Wherefore did Sarah laugh,** saying, **Shall I of
a surety bear a child,** which am old? **Is any thing too hard
for the Lord?** At the time appointed I will return unto thee,
according to the time of life, and Sarah shall have a son.
Then **Sarah denied,** saying, I laughed not; for she was
afraid. And he said, Nay; but thou didst laugh* (Genesis
18:9-15 KJV, emphasis added).

Let's look at this story chronologically. Let's see what happened step by step and apply the valuable lessons to be learned to
our lives.

1. *"Sarah, your wife, will have a son."*—Sarah is eaves-
   dropping on a conversation between her husband
   and the Lord. She overheard God making a promise
   to them concerning having a child.

2. *"Sarah heard it."*—This word was not even intended
   for her ears. God knew that she was not ready to
   receive this heavy revelation. Some people are not yet
   prepared to hear God's revelation for them.

3. *"Abraham and Sarah were old."*—She focused on the
   obvious negative—they were both old. If it had simply been Abraham who was old and her body was

still of child-bearing years, her reaction would not have been disbelief. And if she had been a young woman, her bearing a child would not have been a justifiable miracle.

4. *"It ceased to be with Sarah."*—Sarah considered that she was past not only childbearing years but was in advanced menopause.

5. *"Sarah laughed."*—Never laugh when God promises to give you something better than you have right now.

6. *"Shall I have pleasure?"*—Sarah had become accustomed to the way things were and could not see herself as having the enjoyment of making love to her husband with the expectation of getting pregnant with a child.

7. *"Wherefore did Sarah laugh?"*—God didn't see anything funny.

8. *"Shall I of a surety bear a child?"*—She questioned God's ability. Does this sound familiar? Didn't the serpent question God's word to Adam and Eve?

9. *"Is there anything too hard for the Lord?"*—This was a rhetorical question posed by God to Abraham.

10. *"Sarah denied."*—She compounded her sin of impugning God's word by lying.

*And the Lord visited Sarah as He had said, and **the Lord did unto Sarah as He had spoken.** For Sarah conceived, and bare Abraham a son in his old age, at the set time of which God had spoken to him. And Abraham called the name of his son that was born unto him, whom Sarah bare to him, **Isaac.** And **Abraham circumcised his son Isaac being eight days old,** as God had commanded him. And **Abraham was an hundred years old,** when his son Isaac was born unto him. And **Sarah said, God hath made me to laugh,** so that **all that hear will laugh with me.** And she said, **Who would have said** unto Abraham, that Sarah should have given children suck? For I have born him a son in his old age* (Genesis 21:1-7 KJV).

Let us look at Sarah's change of heart. Now we see that she realizes the appropriate time for laughter was after the promise had come.

1. *"The Lord did unto Sarah as He had spoken."*—God cannot *not* keep His Word.

2. *"Isaac"*—This name literally means laughter, a perpetual reminder that God will cause you to laugh each and every time you behold His promise. The Lord makes unrealistic (by human standards) promises come true.

3. *"Abraham circumcised his son Isaac, being eight days old."*—Whatever God gives you, quickly give it back to Him. This is a sign of your ultimate gratitude. This act will also ensure that God will continually bring supply into your hand.

4. *"Abraham was an hundred years old."*—God waited to the point that not only was his wife certifiably, "out of order" but also Abraham too. This level of absurdity always sets the stage for a genuine miracle.

5. *"Sarah said, God hath made me to laugh."*—This is key. It was obvious that Sarah's first laugh was at God's expense. Her last laugh was at God's goodness. This time Sarah knew to whom she should credit her laughter.

6. *"All that hear will laugh with me."*—Those who had been laughing at Sarah were now going to laugh *with* her. All those who had questioned her and Abraham's promise were going to have to now question their own idea of what was possible and what was impossible. God has an uncanny way of drawing us into His world, a world not limited by natural laws.

7. *"Who would have said"*—One way that we could translate this is simply, "Who would have thought?" That is the king of blessing that God's getting ready to bestow upon you. This kind of blessing will make everyone who sees you ask, "Who would have thought that God could have pulled this one off?" This is the kind of blessing where no one will have any doubt that God and God alone performed the miracle.

If you take nothing more with you, remember this—*Never underestimate the power of God!*

Attitude Really Is Everything

Whatever you do, do not allow your attitude to short circuit your blessing. As someone once said, your attitude will determine your altitude. You have to maintain the right attitude before God and before man if you are going to ascend to the great heights reserved for you. You must act like you believe God is a keeper of His Word, being fully confident that He will come through for you. It's said that your attitude will determine your *altitude* in life. How high you go is directly connected to your mindset, your outlook on life. Think small...live small. You say, "But this is just the way that I am, I've always been this way" Well, change!

I've seen so many folks come so close to seeing their promise manifested only to fall short because they chose to have a horrible attitude. There are women who have become bitter because they were abused by an insensitive man. When that happened they vowed they'd never trust another man ever again. Worse yet, they began to develop the most uncalled for nasty attitude as a self-protection mechanism. Although they thought that the method would save them from hurt, it backfired on them. They had put up such a high wall, that even when God sent His chosen one their way, they could not receive it.

Negative attitudes attract negative people and events. Positive attitudes attract positive people and positive happenings in your life. It's been proven over and over again. We literally attract that which we expect in life.

New York Times best-selling author John Maxwell in his book *The Winning Attitude: Your Key to Personal Success* writes, "Remember, the difficulty really becomes a problem when we internalize unfortunate circumstances. Another thing to remember when the weather gets rough is that what really matters is what happens in us, not to us! When the external circumstances lead to wrong internal reactions, we really have problems. I once talked to a man who was having financial difficulty. He faced the prospect of losing everything. I offered prayer and encouragement during this difficult time. His reaction: 'I've never been closer to God!' He told how this trial was making him stronger in his walk with God."[21]

Maxwell's advice is profoundly true. In his illustration, this man could have chosen to get angry with God and bitter. He could have chosen to ask questions like, "Why is this happening to me?" and "What did I do to deserve this?" Both questions will lead you on a downward spiral to darkness and depression. The way you choose to respond determines the duration and outcome of your trials.

Having survived the nightmare of being forced to live in concentration camps, Victor E. Frankl said of attitude, "Everything can be taken from a man but...the last of the human freedoms— to choose one's attitude in any given set of circumstances, to choose one's own way."[22] This reminds me of a popular message I preached about ten years ago, entitled, "It depends on how you look at it." The whole premise of my message was that there are two ways to look at everything. One way to look at things is through the eyes of the present, those things that will not last because they are only temporary. To give an unprecedented amount of attention to that which is not going last anyway is a terrible waste of time, energy, and resources.

The other way to look at things is from its eternal point of view; you will always be inclined to invest into that which has lasting value. Your attitude will be based on how you look at things. You can look at being fired from your job as the worst thing that ever happened to you. Or you can look at being fired as God setting you up for a much-needed promotion. One person may want to end his or her life after discovering that their spouse wants a divorce. Another person, although saddened by the decision to divorce, may look at the same situation as an opportunity to wholeheartedly devote themselves to the work of the Lord.

A mother may cry profusely after hearing that her only son has to serve a mandatory ten-year sentence for drug trafficking. Another mother facing the same situation with her son may look at imprisonment as a blessing from God, knowing that now her child is safer than if he were on the streets. Also, she might realize that prison may be the only place where God can actually get a message through to him. *It all depends on how you look at it.*

For our light affliction, which is but for a moment, worketh for us a far more exceeding and eternal weight of glory; While we look not at the things which are seen, but at the things which are not seen: for the things which are seen are temporal; but the things which are not seen are eternal (2 Corinthians 4:17-18 KJV).

I'm Looking Forward to Laughing

She is clothed with strength and dignity; she can laugh at the days to come (Proverbs 31:25).

You ought to be rejoicing right now. You may not be laughing now but you *will* laugh in the days to come. In fact, you will be laughing all the way to the bank. Your day will come, and you will have everything.

On your way there, you'll be laughing right past your creditors, past backbiters, past liars, and past violators. In a moment you are going to start looking forward to laughing. Because you are realizing that when you laugh, your laughter sends out a strong message, a clarion cry, that everything that you went through has paid off, big time.

Weeping may last through the night but joy comes in the morning!

Chapter 7

Is There Anything Too Hard for God?

And the Lord said unto Abraham, Wherefore did Sarah laugh, saying, Shall I of a surety bear a child, which am old? Is any thing too hard for the Lord? At the time appointed I will return unto thee, according to the time of life, and Sarah shall have a son. Then Sarah denied, saying, I laughed not; for she was afraid. And He said, Nay; but thou didst laugh (Genesis 18:13-15 KJV).

Then came the word of the Lord unto Jeremiah, saying, Behold, I am the Lord, the God of all flesh: is there any thing too hard for Me? (Jeremiah 32:26-27 KJV).

could not complete this work without having a chapter solely dedicated to talking about an all-powerful God. Much of Christendom, even in antiquity, has made man the center of the faith for many centuries. Now, I understand why the Church leaned in this direction. Life in general can be so taxing, so arduous that we tend to need much consolation and attention; and then we begin to believe that everything should be about us. In short, life has really done a great job at damaging us. So a "gospel" that focuses primarily on us is convenient and therapeutic for believers. But when we leave God at the edges of our life, we lose our most important message that life can only be lived by His power and grace. It is not all about you. It is about Him!

Prior to the recent praise and worship revolution, most of the songs that were sung in our churches revolved around us, not God. Let me clarify my point. I totally understand why Africans and African Americans needed to sing the slave songs and Negro spirituals. They relied on those songs for sustenance for their souls, their daily bread. The rigors and consistent hostile treatment they endured daily in their role as slaves left them with little hope or consolation and singing of a better place helped get them through.

So even though the words were not necessarily freeing and liberating words, they sufficed. They did not have a command of the English language, knew few words, because they were not allowed education. When a person's words are limited, their lyrics will be limited also. That was their case. However, we've held on to the same kinds of songs for far too long now.

I can understand singing those songs as a reminder of how far we've come. But those songs do not glorify God, but rather embellish an age-old problem. Two of the songs listed below are just a few of many songs that magnify our trouble, focus more on us, and less on God. These songs are not bad songs, but they are not the best songs particularly for the times that we live in.

Jesus Will Fix It
(Words and music: Traditional Spiritual)[23]

Lyrics:

Trouble in my way (Trouble in my way)
Have to cry sometime (I have to cry sometime)
Trouble in my way (Trouble in my way)
Have to cry sometime (I have to cry sometime)
Lay awake at night (Lay awake at night)
But that's all right (That's all right).

Chorus 1:

I know that Jesus (Jesus, He will fix it)
I know that Jesus (Jesus, He will fix it)
I know that Jesus (Jesus, He will fix it)
After a while (After a while).

Nobody Knows De Trouble I've Seen[24]
(Negro Spiritual)

Nobody knows de trouble I've seen
Nobody knows de trouble but Jesus
Nobody knows de trouble I've seen
Glory Hallelujah!

Sometimes I'm up, sometimes I'm down
Oh, yes, Lord
Sometimes I'm almost to de groun'
Oh, yes, Lord

Although you see me goin' 'long so
Oh, yes, Lord
I have my trials here below
Oh, yes, Lord

If you get there before I do
Oh, yes, Lord
Tell all-a my friends I'm coming too
Oh, yes, Lord.

Nobody knew the trouble that the slaves were seeing. We have different struggles today that are systemic and may stem from those days, but cannot be shared as our contemporary personal experience. For example, I would rather sing songs about living my life in Him, enjoying the experiences of freedom in Christ, and letting Him know how much I love Him. I'd prefer to spend most of my praise and worship time just catching up on thanking God for the last thing He did for me. We've become so enamored with those types of songs that some of us have forgotten how to praise Him for His mighty works and beneficent deeds.

O Sovereign Lord, You have begun to show to Your servant Your greatness and Your strong hand. For what god is there in Heaven or on earth who can do the deeds and mighty works You do? (Deuteronomy 3:24).

Sometimes we become so focused on our problems that we lose focus on the "God Who Is There" and is able to sustain us and strengthen us through all our troubles. It would seem that declaring God's credentials would help to strengthen your faith in Him, recognizing that God does not have any limitations, especially when it concerns you. God will go to great lengths to prove Himself strong and mighty in your eyes. He has done it countless times before, and He will do it again when given the proper atmosphere conducive to miracles.

God is the central point of everything. Everything that is, is in Him. Everything that was, came out of Him. The Bible says in Romans 13:1 (KJV), "*Let every soul be subject unto the higher powers. For there is no power but of God: the powers that be are ordained of God.*" There is not power but of God—it is easy to lose sight of this powerful truth. Everything that we will ever need is in Him, He being the solution to all of our mortal and spiritual concerns. Noted German theologian and scholar, Paul Tillich, sheds his insight on this topic of God:

> God is the answer to the question implied in man's finitude; He is the name for that which concerns man ultimately. This does not mean that first there is a being called God and then the demand that man should be ultimately concerned about him. It means that whatever concerns a man ultimately becomes god for him, and, conversely, it means that a man can be concerned ultimately only about that which is god for him.[25]

Does God Have Limitations?

As a child, I grew up hearing songs declaring the power of God and the awesomeness of God. The songs, the worship, the preaching, all aided in helping me to form my own personal philosophy of why I love Him so dearly. Not only as a child but also as an adult, I've been fascinated by how God shows off His matchless power, and how He has a personal interest in the lives of His people.

I've always been fascinated by great thinkers and great minds. Thinkers ask questions. And questions provoke thought. I've always believed that the true Christian experience was deeply entrenched in thought. We have been detached from the great writings of the great theologians like Paul Tillich, Karl Barth, and Dietrich Bonhoeffer.

Many Eastern religious traditions focus a great deal on meditation that is a concentrated form of reflective thought. Most Christians have never read any of the writings of Madame Guyon or St. John of the Cross. Sad to say, there are few Christians who have embraced this age-old spiritual tradition of meditating even though the Scriptures are replete with commands to do so.

The writings of these great men and women of God attest to the magnificence and power of God. Their writings inspire us to new heights. Unfortunately most of us are so caught up in the activities of our daily lives that we do not make room for the inspiration found in these works. They would create new pictures in our mind—pictures painted by their words describing the greatness of God.

Does God have any limitations? First, we all need to understand that one of God's eternal attributes is that He is Holy. His holiness may be far different from what you've been taught. When I speak of His Holiness, I am not talking about doctrines, and I am not talking about a particular dress code. I am not talking about how we have degraded the meaning of holiness.

His Holiness means that He is in a class by Himself. He is different than, separate from, and distinctly unique from anyone else in the universe. So if there were anyone who can truthfully claim such a lofty declaration as, "Nothing is too hard for Me," it would be God, since He has no peers.

He is omnipotent—the *all*-mighty and *all*-powerful God.

He is omnipresent—present everywhere at the same time.

He is omniscient—knowing all things, past, present, and future.

If these theological truths are real then that means that our God is able to take care of you. He has the power! Neither you nor your circumstances can put any limit on His power. He transcends all things.

Anything that opposes God's Holiness is diametrically opposed to His nature. For example, it is impossible for God to lie. The Scriptures say, *"Paul, a servant of God, and an apostle of Jesus Christ, according to the faith of God's elect, and the acknowledging of the truth which is after godliness; in hope of eternal life, which God, that cannot lie, promised before the world began"* (Titus 1:1-2 KJV). God cannot lie—it would work against His very nature and that is not possible. If God lied, He would no longer be God. If God makes a promise then He will not go back on His promise, and He has the power to fulfill His promise.

God Is Spirit

God is a Spirit: and they that worship Him must worship Him in spirit and in truth (John 4:24 KJV).

God is spirit. That is His nature, and the Scriptures say that God created us in His image. Man was created spirit, soul, and body. Because man has a spirit he is unique among all of God's creation. Man's spirit enables him to be able to hear and experience God.

It took two independent ingredients to bring life to man—body and spirit. As spirit was breathed into man's body, he came to life. The soul was the consequential product of man's body coming into contact with the spirit of the living God. The soul with its mind, will, and emotions is the image of God.

The breath of God was the catalyst for the creation of man. This celestial fluid gave him life, enabling him to live in a new dimension. It opened the door for man to be transported into the realm of God. In this dimension called spirit, man would communicate and know fellowship with God.

Without the spirit, the life of the soul is diminished as it sinks into darkness. As long as man's spirit is alive, he could live above the natural realm and soar into spiritual realms and fellowship with his Creator. This is what sets man apart from the rest of creation. The image of the Creator was massaged into the DNA of the created being making him unique among all God's creation. The image of God in man, in the living soul, sets him apart. S.D. Gordon, in his book, *Quiet Talks About Jesus*, wrote these dynamic words. "The very life of man is a bit of God. Man is of the essence of God. Every man is the presence-chamber of God."[26]

Why does all of this matter? It means that God is fully capable of solving *any* problem that you may face. The key word in the last sentence is *any*. Because of who He is and how He has created you, there is the possibility of God resolving every problem in your life. We are not alone. God is with us and God has created others like us who will make our world a better place. There are those who have gone before us who have paved a spiritual highway for us—all made possible by the One who loves you.

No Job Too Large or Small

What qualifies you to experience God's power in your life? You won't find the answer in religion. The answer is your weakness. Most people think that if they could get their life together then God would show up in their lives. What they don't know is that God wants to show up in their lives so that He can reform their lives. If you could do it, then you obviously wouldn't need God. It doesn't matter how seemingly small or how overwhelming the problem, God waits for us to do everything we possibly can, until we have exhausted all our resources, until we come to an understanding of our destitution—then He steps in.

You would only hire a plumber to tackle jobs that you were incapable or ill-equipped to perform. It is no different with God.

He is the answer to any problem that we will face, but He wants to make sure that we can't help the situation ourselves first. God wants to ensure that when the victory has been won, He will get all of the glory.

Even in the case of Abraham, God waited to make sure that Abraham and Sarah would not be capable of bearing children. They wouldn't need Viagra or some modern cloning technique. If they had been able to do what was necessary to conceive a child, where would the miracle have been? Don't rob God of the miracle He has for you by trying to resolve your own issues.

Then He took the five loaves and the two fishes, and looking up to heaven, He blessed them, and brake, and gave to the disciples to set before the multitude (Luke 9:16 KJV).

Jesus' disciples must have turned and looked at each other in disbelief when, after praying over this small lunch, Jesus told them to serve the people! Was He kidding? I think they may have even laughed. Maybe He was pulling their leg. That amount of food could never feed 5,000. But, folks, we're talking a miracle! We're talking Jesus! God loves to create scenarios where anyone looking on would declare, "Ridiculous!" He loves to surprise us by making our impossibilities become possible by the touch of the Master's hand.

God wanted to make sure that the amount was so ridiculously small that people would have to laugh when they heard, "Jesus is gonna turn this little boy's lunch into a feast for thousands." Go ahead and laugh. It sounds funny. It doesn't make any sense at all.

But that's the kind of stuff that God loves to do. Look at what Jesus does in the Scripture below.

The Power of Influence

And He suffered no man to follow Him, save Peter, and James, and John the brother of James. And He cometh to the house of the ruler of the synagogue, and seeth the tumult, and them that wept and wailed greatly. And when He was come in, He saith unto them, Why make ye this ado, and weep? the damsel is not dead, but sleepeth. And they laughed Him to scorn. But when He had put them all out, He taketh the father and the mother of the damsel, and them that were with Him, and entereth in where the damsel was lying. And He took the damsel by the hand, and said unto her, Talitha cumi; which is, being interpreted, Damsel, I say unto thee, arise. And straightway the damsel arose, and walked; for she was of the age of twelve years. And they were astonished with a great astonishment (Mark 5:37-42 KJV).

What is more impossible than raising someone from the dead? No situation is more final than when life departs from a child. And the people reacted as most of us would today, if we had never seen such a thing—*they laughed him to scorn.* They had no idea that the laws of nature did not apply to this Man.

Something I want you to notice about this account: Jesus only took three of His disciples with Him. Jesus only allowed Peter, James, and John to accompany Him on this mission. He had 12 disciples at the time and thousands of devoted followers. Yet for this kind of miracle-working, only a certain kind of person could be present.

This is a message for you. The blessing that God is getting ready to pour out on you and through you is so amazing, it will require you to exclude certain people from your inner circle. You've got to *fire some folks* if you expect this blessing to occur. You ask, "What kind of people do I need to exclude from my circle?" Anyone who does not believe. *All* the doubters have to go. Notice Thomas was not invited to this raising from the dead ceremony. What is Thomas remembered for? His nickname: "Doubting Thomas."

Your blessing could have been held up now for years because you have surrounded yourself with people who really do not believe that you should be blessed. If they don't feel blessed, they certainly don't want you to receive a blessing. You've ignorantly joined yourself to people who have limiting beliefs. And their *limiting beliefs* have rubbed off on you to the point that you too now have limited God to what you can see and what you can understand.

So you have got to let them know that they are not invited. Only those who believe that your life should be and will be greater than it is now can come and witness the miraculous hand of God. Jesus approaches the house of the ruler and finds everyone weeping and wailing because this girl has died. Jesus asks them what all the fuss is about. The child is only sleeping. I think at that point they must have thought Jairus had invited some madman to his home. How could He not see the girl was *dead*? They began to laugh until they could hardly catch their breath.

That is what people will do when you, confident in your union with God, declare things that are not as though they were.

The State of Your Union

What is the state of your union with God? The state of your union is always what God says and not what you are experiencing. Your circumstances do not determine your real position. Though men may reject you, God will not. Men's rejection is simply an opportunity for God to demonstrate His acceptance of you. You could have just been fired from your job, not knowing how you are going to pay your bills. But because you are united with Christ, His pronouncement over your life is the final say, the *last word*, as it were. Jesus says you are going to lead your own company, making quarterly profits of more than $15 million. To those looking on, the thinking is, "You are crazy! You just lost your job and have debts that need to be paid." They begin laughing you to scorn— to relegate you. All that really doesn't matter. Whether your friends and family get the point or see where you are heading, has no relevance. When God speaks, it is done! A chain of events is set in motion that is going to bring that word to pass. And once set in motion, they cannot be reversed.

Stay Focused

Notice that Jesus did not even respond to their laughing. Which brings me to my next point: You've got to stay focused. Their laughing (at the wrong time) is an assignment from hell to distract you and make you feel as if God's words are debatable. Pay no attention to those who say, "God's not going to do that for *you*. You'll never live *there*. They'll never hire *you*. Your son received a 20-year sentence; he'll *never* see the light of day." The list goes on and on. Let them laugh. You stay focused on the promise.

Jesus said to the dead little girl, "*Talitha cumi,*" "Little girl, arise." In other words, "Get up; you've been sleeping long enough." Are there some areas in your life that have been lying dormant for much too long now? Is there some area of wealth that you stopped pursuing because you thought that it was dead?

Are there relationships that you allowed to dissolve that were ordained of God for your development and growth? What about those dreams that you knew were from God that you once shared with your so-called friends, and they extinguished your exuberance and enthusiasm to pursue them? God is saying to you, "Get up!" Get up now and allow God to not only perform a miracle, but to make you become a living miracle!

How God Works

Since you've gone through so much embarrassment, God wants to make it up to you by going to the extreme. That's how He works. I've provided a graph below, giving you a few examples of how God will bring you from one extreme to another. He is an *extremist*. So if you are in an extremely bad condition, start rejoicing because God is getting ready to bring you to an extremely favorable place.

After the first chart you will see a second chart, in which I've intentionally left the boxes empty to give you the opportunity to write your life. Where are you now? Write that down. What is the extreme opposite of your present situation? Write it down. Where you are now—they're laughing at you. Where you are going to be—you'll be laughing at the hilarity of His works in your life.

From One Extreme	To the Other Extreme
Homeless	Owning an apartment complex
Nelson Mandela was imprisoned for his stand against apartheid.	Mandela became the President of South Africa.
Joseph was sold out by his brothers and lived in a pit and a prison.	Joseph became the governor of Egypt.
Jesus was rejected by His own people.	Jesus became the Chief Cornerstone.
Jesus died.	He has risen.

From One Extreme	To the Other Extreme
_____	_____
_____	_____
_____	_____
_____	_____
_____	_____

Thou hast caused men to ride over our heads; we went through fire and through water: but Thou broughtest us out into a wealthy place (Psalm 66:12 KJV).

Chapter 8

The Ridiculous Blessing

My mother told me I was blessed, and I have always taken her word for it. Being born of—or reincarnated from—royalty is nothing like being blessed. Royalty is inherited from another human being, blessedness comes from God.[27]

—Duke Ellington

The hardest arithmetic to master is that which enables us to count our blessings.[28]

—Eric Hofler

Reflect upon your present blessings of which every man has many—not on your past misfortunes, of which all men have some.[29]

—Charles Dickens

idiculous blessing—the showers of blessings that fall from Heaven every day upon our lives are absurd. The blessings that come to us are not based upon who we are or what we do. They are based upon who He is. We live in a culture where reward is based upon effort. You don't get something for nothing. But in God's Kingdom the economics of the world are turned upside down and reward is based upon the Giver.

Normally when one uses the word *ridiculous*, you think of something silly or a type of foolish jesting. While this is a part of the word, one cannot stop there because there is more meaning yet to be discovered. Merriam Webster's Unabridged Dictionary defines ridiculous:

- fit or likely to excite ridicule : unworthy of serious consideration : absurd, comical, funny, laughable, preposterous

- dialect—violating decency or moral sense: indecent, outrageous, scandalous, synonyms see laughable

There are three words that strike me in this definition and that are relevant to the theme of ridiculous blessing:

1. Indecent

2. Outrageous

3. Scandalous

Indecent Blessing

The blessing that God has in store for you is indecent by others' standards. What is indecent? Morally offensive, improper. Indecency is generally determined by a standard upheld by society that determines what is not ethical for you to have or for you to do. It is improper and offensive that God should be so extravagant in His love for us.

If God provided you with a new car, let's say a Mercedes-Benz, a Lexus, a Maserati, or even a Rolls Royce Phantom, most Christians would say that this is indecent, morally unethical for a Christian to own. Now, it's not that the thing is indecent or even that it has an unethical quality to it; it's just the people's view of it. Or if God blesses you with a French chateau, many people in the same group would immediately start complaining that nobody needs to have a house that big.

But interestingly enough, none of those people seemed to express any genuine concern when you did not have a car to drive at all or when you were renting a small apartment or homeless. Frankly speaking, they can keep their views to themselves. A long time ago, I stopped making excuses about His blessings on my life. "God, in any way You see fit to bless me, I receive it." So be prepared—the blessing that God is preparing for you will be one that will attract major attention from the critics; so much so that you will be ridiculed for your blessing. Your blessing won't qualify as a ridiculous blessing, until you've been *ridiculed* first.

The stuff that you have that everyone's glad about and praising you for is not the ridiculous blessing that God is trying to get to you. No, it's the stuff that everybody on your block, half the people in your family, and many of your so-called friends will ridicule you for having.

Outrageous Blessing

Your blessing will cause people to become outraged. I've seen it happen in my own life. People that were once cool with me began acting funny when God started blessing me real good. Some folks became outraged, downright fuming at my success. People began lying about me, talking behind my back, and some even tried to hurt me. All I knew, through the process of watching their behavior, was that I had just received an authentic God blessing, one that caused people to become incensed.

For a while, I could never understand why people would be so mad about my blessing. I've never had a problem with other people's blessing. But when God gives the ridiculous blessing, it seems to make folks mad. The blessing is so significant that it makes people jealous that you received it, and not them. Everywhere God is, is a place of abundance, for God is an abundant God. If God is in you, then you are a person of abundance and that abundance is outrageous, and it creates outrage in others.

The aphorisms of Jesus reflect this outrageous nature of God. In the message of Jesus, the last shall be first. The least shall be the greatest, and the lost shall be found.

Scandalous Blessing

Another angle of looking at ridiculous is by considering the word scandalous. The ridiculous blessing is scandalous. Scandalous is when your views or action directly confronts the conventional moral or spiritual views. Jesus Christ was scandalous. You say, how can you attribute such a defamatory word to our Lord and Savior? I am completely convinced that if Jesus were here in the flesh that He would be proud to accept the title and would wear it as a badge of honor.

All throughout the New Testament we see Jesus getting caught up in scandalous activity. He violated Sabbaths, ruined established businesses, allowed women to touch Him that were ceremonially unclean, and even committed blasphemy by calling Himself the Son of God. His entire ministry was marked with scandal. His fame spread abroad not necessarily for the good that He did, but rather for His scandalous involvement in the affairs of men. You know that negative news spreads a whole lot faster than good news. Jesus is so amazing. Most people who are accused of scandalous activity are usually brought down within a short period of time. Not so with Jesus, people wanted to know how a righteous man could be so scandalous, yet righteous at the same time.

And He entered again into the synagogue; and there was a man there which had a withered hand. And they watched Him, whether He would heal Him on the sabbath day; that they might accuse Him. And He saith unto the man which had the withered hand, Stand forth. And He saith unto them, Is it lawful to do good on the sabbath days, or to do evil? to save life, or to kill? But they held their peace. And when He had looked round about on them with anger, being grieved for the hardness of their hearts, He saith unto the man, Stretch forth thine hand. And he stretched it out: and his hand was restored whole as the other (Mark 3:1-5 KJV).

Here, again, we see Jesus in the middle of a scandalous affair. Being a Jewish person and a student of the Mosaic Law, Christ knew far better than anyone exactly what the law prohibited and what it allowed. But when it came to a situation that had to do with life and death, or just the quality of life that a person enjoyed, Jesus disregarded the written law to exercise what He knew as the higher law—the Law of Life.

When it would help a person to live better or to live longer, Jesus would suspend the rules set in place to show off His grace toward humanity. That was the situation in this narrative. Jesus entered the synagogue. He notices a man with an emaciated hand, all shrunken and crippled. Not only was it obvious that this man's hand was shriveled, it was also obvious that this man's hand could not function, rendering it useless. It was just an extension of his body but had no functionality. Jesus is the author of the "Law of Use," and He knew how meaningless life could be if this law was not actively engaged.

If this man could not use his hand, there would be so many things that he would not be able to enjoy or to participate in, simple things like bathing, eating, writing, catching, shaking hands, and carrying objects. He, just like others, deserved a chance to be able to fully utilize his hands. So when Jesus saw this man He wanted to immediately express His heartfelt compassion toward him by healing him.

The only problem was: He was healing the man on the Sabbath. And the Law forbade anyone from performing any such activity on that day. For Jesus to pull this one off, He would have to do something ridiculous, something scandalous by religious standards. He would have to break the Law. In so doing, He knew that He could be arrested and charged with violating the Jewish law. But restoring this man to wholeness was far more important to Jesus than any consequences He might have to face.

The Pharisees stood by watching intently to see whether Jesus would heal the man, looking and hoping for an opportunity to bring accusations against Him. Well, they got exactly what they were wishing for. Jesus healed the man as expected. Again, you must realize how Jesus thinks. The ridiculous blessing is more important than what people may think or say. If you are the kind of person who is afraid to hear the criticisms of others, then you don't qualify for the ridiculous blessing.

You've got to be ready for the army of accusers ready to hurl their accusations at you without being shaken by their words. Little did the people know that Jesus was the reason why the Sabbath was created in the first place. So if the Sabbath was created for His glory, then healing on the Sabbath would only bring more glory to the Lord. And getting glory is something that God never passes up. So if your situation seems outrageously indecent and utterly hopeless, then you are a prime candidate for the ridiculous blessing, the one that Jesus performs personally.

And he said unto them, That the Son of man is Lord also of the Sabbath (Luke 6:5 KJV).

A Ridiculous Command,
Ridiculous Obedience, a Ridiculous Supply

And Elijah the Tishbite, who was of the inhabitants of Gilead, said unto Ahab, As the Lord God of Israel liveth, before whom I stand, there shall not be dew nor rain these years, but according to my word. And the word of the Lord came unto him, saying,

Get thee hence, and turn thee eastward, and hide thyself by the brook Cherith, that is before Jordan. And it shall be, that thou shalt drink of the brook; and I have commanded the ravens to feed thee there. So he went and did according unto the word of the Lord: for he went and dwelt by the brook Cherith, that is before Jordan. And the ravens brought him bread and flesh in the morning, and bread and flesh in the evening; and he drank of the brook. And it came to pass after a while, that the brook dried up, because there had been no rain in the land. And the word of the Lord came unto him, saying, Arise, get thee to Zarephath, which belongeth to Zidon, and dwell there: behold, I have commanded a widow woman there to sustain thee. So he arose and went to Zarephath. And when he came to the gate of the city, behold, the widow woman was there gathering of sticks: and he called to her, and said, Fetch me, I pray thee, a little water in a vessel, that I may drink. And as she was going to fetch it, he called to her, and said, Bring me, I pray thee, a morsel of bread in thine hand. And she said, As the Lord thy God liveth, I have not a cake, but an handful of meal in a barrel, and a little oil in a cruse: and, behold, I am gathering two sticks, that I may go in and dress it for me and my son, that we may eat it, and die. And Elijah said unto her, Fear not; go and do as thou hast said: but make me thereof a little cake first, and bring it unto me, and after make for thee and for thy son.

For thus saith the Lord God of Israel, The barrel of meal shall not waste, neither shall the cruse of oil fail, until the day that the Lord sendeth rain upon the earth. And she went and did according to the saying of Elijah: and she, and he, and her house, did eat many days. And the barrel of meal wasted not, neither did the cruse of oil fail, according to the word of the Lord, which he spake by Elijah (1 Kings 17:1-16 KJV).

The story of the widow woman in First Kings 17:1-16 is a remarkable story worth thoughtful consideration. The text lists all kinds of ridiculous moments that would ultimately lead to the most ridiculous, unheard of blessings. There are three things that happen in this text that you and I can gain much from. It starts with a ridiculous command from the Lord, and continues with ridiculous obedience that facilitates ridiculous blessings. And the cycle continues all throughout the story. I could not pass up the opportunity to comment on these ridiculous reactions.

1. *"As the Lord God of Israel liveth, before whom I stand, there shall not be dew nor rain"*—**A ridiculous prophecy.** In our modern day, when prophets generally prophesy what we want to hear, it is difficult to fully appreciate a prophet like Elijah, one who will forthrightly declare the Word of the Lord even though it may be unconventional. What king would

want to hear that his kingdom was going to experience a drought? Realize how ridiculous this prophecy was. In some ways, this word from the Lord could have caused the king to arrest the prophet immediately for speaking such a curse over His kingdom. But he didn't, and the word of the Lord spoken through Elijah came to pass.

2. *"Get thee hence, and turn thee eastward, and hide thyself by the brook Cherith."*—**A ridiculous command.** God often gives orders first and reasons after. He told Elijah to go to a place that he had never been before, and to locate a brook called Cherith. That's it. God never feels obligated to give all of the information up front. He will give you commands in bits and pieces. When you obey the first command you qualify to receive the next command. If however, you do not obey the first command, you will inevitably continue to repeat it until you get it right.

3. *"I have commanded the ravens to feed thee there."*—**A ridiculous command.** It has always been a matter of wonder exactly how Elijah was fed while at the brook Cherith. The very thought of a raven, which is such an unclean and avaricious bird, being commanded to feed the prophet is an absurdity of great proportion. The real difficulty here is that we see again God giving a command that does not make sense to the natural mind. But even more incredible is the fact that God does not give this task to a human agent, but to a bird. This goes to show you once again that God causes the most unlikely beings to do the most

unlikely things on behalf of His chosen people, all at the sound of His word.

4. *"So he went and did according unto the word of the Lord."*—**Ridiculous obedience.** Get in the habit of doing whatever God tells you to do and do it without hesitation!

5. *"The brook dried up...Arise, get thee to Zarephath."*— **A ridiculous command.** Don't stay where you are after your brook has dried up. When your brook dries, it's time to move on. Many people find it hard to move on, even though there is no longer any reason to stay where they are. So God gives Elijah a directive to go somewhere else that is unknown to him. God will often cause you to explore uncharted territory, for it is there that your blessing lies.

6. *"I have commanded a widow woman there to sustain thee. So he arose and went."*—**Ridiculous obedience.** He did not second guess God's word. He just obeyed, trusting God had a plan.

7. *"Bring me, I pray thee, a morsel of bread in thine hand."*—**A ridiculous request.** God often asks us to do those things we think we cannot do. This has to be the most ridiculous request of them all. This woman was completely broke, financially, spiritually, emotionally, and physically. She was hungry. She had only enough food for her and her son to eat. After which, she expected to die from starvation.

8. *"Fear not; go and do as thou hast said: but make me thereof a little cake first, and bring it unto me."*—**A ridiculous command.** After the prophet listened to her reason why she could not do what he asked of her, he simply repeated his request but now with a twist. He asked her to give him his portion *first.* Though she didn't realize it, her first fruits offering would be a down payment on the perpetual supply that her act of obedience would spawn.

9. *"The barrel of meal shall not waste, neither shall the cruse of oil fail, until the day."*—**A ridiculous prophecy.** Again we see a lofty word. What he is saying never happened for anyone anywhere that she knew of. How can a cruse of oil stay full? How can a barrel of meal never decrease unless someone continually fills it up? This makes no sense.

10. *"She went."*—**Ridiculous obedience.** Do what He says to do!

11. *"And she, and he, and her house, did eat many days."*—*A ridiculous blessing.* God is faithful!

One of the major impediments to our receiving a ridiculous blessing is that we try too hard to make sense of what God is doing in our lives. We want to be certain that if He gives us a command, a prophecy, or if He asks something of us, that we are able to understand it. If understanding everything is your prerequisite for obeying the Lord, you might as well quit right *now.* You are not going to always understand everything. But if you just do whatever He asks of you in faith and obedience, God will move Heaven and earth to bring you your blessing. You have to keep the dream alive and have faith in the outrageous God.

How Ridiculous Can God Really Get?

To the extent that you've gone through your pain, to that same extent *God's gonna make you laugh*. The enemy has done a number on your mind trying to convince you that the ridiculous blessing is no more than pie in the sky for naïve folk with a fantastical dream. Don't buy into his lie! He doesn't want you to actualize how great your life will be after the Lord has come through for you. Satan knows that as your faith in Jesus grows, his attacks and accusations will lose their power over you.

So if you are homeless, when that pendulum swings, you are going to be walking into your new home. Your car may be repossessed, but when the pendulum swings, you are going to own a leasing service, and as the Lord leads you, you're going to be the one giving cars to other folks in need. At this end of the pendulum swing, it may appear your children are totally out of control, dishonoring God and everything that is holy. But when it swings back each one of them will be saved and serving God in the places He seeds them. Get ready! God's pendulum is about to swing in your life.

When Do the Blessings End?

In those days, and in that time, saith the Lord, the children of Israel shall come, they and the children of Judah together, *going and weeping: they shall go, and seek the Lord their God. They shall ask the way to Zion with their faces thitherward, saying, Come, and let us join ourselves to the Lord in a **perpetual covenant** that shall not be forgotten* (Jeremiah 50:4-5 KJV, emphasis added).

The blessing of the Lord, it maketh rich, and He addeth no sorrow with it (Proverbs 10:22 KJV).

According to God's Word, your blessings do not have an expiration date. You have a *perpetual* covenant, that is, "continuing without interruption." When God makes a person become rich, it is totally different from the person who becomes rich by fraudulent methods, illegal schemes, and dishonest means. God's riches never come with sorrow or grief. God does not bless us so we can hoard our blessings. He prospers us so that we might be a blessing to the whole earth. And until He sees that heart within us, our blessing will be on hold.

I've got a question for you. When do you think it is fair and reasonable to be cut out of your family's inheritance? Or if you have children, at what point do you believe you should stop blessing them? That might seem like a foolish question to you. But how much more foolish is it to think that God would tease us with His blessings? First, He holds them just out of our reach, and then He finally gives them to us, only to then turn around and snatch them away. That is not our God! He is not a sadistic father who gets his kicks out of tormenting his kids. When God wants to bless you, only you can hold up or turn off the outpouring of God's blessings on your life.

Only your doubt and disbelief can interrupt the flow of His blessings. Your attitude, your confessions, and your thoughts all play a vital part in opening and closing the floodgates of His blessing on your life. Our God delights in bestowing good gifts on His kids. He finds great joy in your coming to Him and asking as a little child who knows his father adores him, for the things you have need of. If you think that the blessing that you've experienced so far is good, if you think you've received some good gifts from Father, you ain't seen nothin' yet!

Chapter 9

God Is a
Covenant-Keeping God

May God give you...For every storm a rainbow, for every tear a smile, for every care a promise and a blessing in each trial. For every problem life sends, a faithful friend to share, for every sigh a sweet song and an answer for each prayer.

—Irish Blessing

God's whole dealing with mankind has been based upon His promises and His faithfulness to come through on His promises no matter the circumstances. It's all about His *covenant*. In order for you to receive a blessing beyond your ability to understand, Hebrews 11:6 says you must believe that God is and that He rewards those who diligently seek Him.

There are many instances all throughout the Scriptures, both Old and New Testament, where God made unconditional covenants with His people that could not be broken. Each time He made a covenant with someone, and when His Word came to fruition, it only helped to strengthen the faith of the people with whom He made the covenant. Sadly, the children of Israel were often distracted by idol worship. Despite the fact that God continually kept His promise to them, they continued to break theirs with Him, causing an unstable relationship between God and Israel.

Nonetheless, God continued to express His desire to keep His covenant regardless of their irresponsible behavior. His nature would not allow Him to abandon His word. This biblical truth shows us how His covenant is not necessarily based upon our commitment or even our sympathy with God's covenant; it is based upon His Word. Please don't run with that statement, misinterpreting my point. I am not suggesting that you and I are allowed to break our covenant with God. We are obligated to carry through on our end of the agreement. However, should we fail to hold up our part, it does not nullify God's faithfulness. He is still bound, by His very nature, to keep His Word. He is bound to you and committed to your success. Others will come and go in your life, but God will always be there cheering you on.

Characteristics of a Covenant

Covenant means "an agreement that is usually formal, solemn, and intended as binding."

In simple words, a *covenant* is "a promise of intent." A covenant is an agreement between two parties or two groups of people that normally, but not always, requires promises on the part of each party to the other and includes their ability to keep their word. The notion of covenant between God and His people is the most fundamental building block of the Scriptures. It is the foundation of the ancient cultures. When God made His covenant with Abraham, He vowed to bless his descendants and to make them His own unique people. It was a covenant initiated by God and motivated by His love for man.

Abraham had a responsibility in the covenant also. He was expected to remain loyal and obedient to God that he might become a living conduit through which God might bless all mankind. "*Now the Lord had said unto Abram, Get thee out of thy country, and from thy kindred, and from thy father's house, unto a land that I will shew thee: And I will make of thee a great nation, and I will bless thee, and make thy name great; and thou shalt be a blessing: And I will bless them that bless thee, and curse him that curseth thee: and in thee shall all families of the earth be blessed*" (Gen. 12:1-3 KJV).

While Abraham is considered the father of faith and God's covenant with him is the most well-known of the biblical covenants, God had established a covenant with Noah long before Abraham lived. God promised Noah that He would never again destroy the world by flood. Then there was a covenant between God and David, in which God promised David that his offspring would be the heirs to the throne of the nation of Israel. "*And when thy days be fulfilled, and thou shalt sleep with thy fathers, I will set up thy seed after thee, which shall proceed out of thy bowels, and I will establish his kingdom. He shall build an house for My name, and I will establish the throne of his kingdom for ever"* (2 Sam. 7:12-13 KJV).

The consummation of this covenant with David was reached when Jesus, a direct descendant of the line of King David, was born in Bethlehem some thousand years after God made this promise to him. This was the fulfillment of "Messianic prophecy."

A covenant, from God's point of view, goes far deeper than simply signing a contract or entering into a verbal agreement. If I were to sign a contract today for someone to do a service for me, that contract would have both a start and ending date written on it.

Covenants differ in that while they do have a very clear starting point, they are usually open-ended. Most covenants are perpetual and continue throughout the posterity of the one with whom the covenant was made. Another distinction is that whereas a contract usually deals with one area of a person's life—their work—a covenant is much like a full coverage insurance policy. It extends to cover a person's entire being, and often their entire family.

The Hebrew root of the word *covenant* literally means "to cut." For this reason people would literally pass through the openly slashed bodies of slain animals after entering into an agreement with each other. This was their way of physically and spiritually demonstrating their wholehearted commitment to the covenant. *"And I will give the men that have transgressed My covenant, which have not performed the words of the covenant which they had made before Me, when they cut the calf in twain, and passed between the parts thereof"* (Jer. 34:18 KJV).

Old Testament covenants were always ratified by shedding of blood, particularly when the covenants were established between two people. God commanded Abraham and his male children to be circumcised as a sign of their covenant with Him. *"This is My covenant, which ye shall keep, between Me and you and thy seed after thee; every man child among you shall be circumcised. And ye shall circumcise the flesh of your foreskin; and it shall be a token of the covenant betwixt Me and you"* (Gen. 17:10-11 KJV).

Even Moses sprinkled the blood of animals on the altar and upon the people who entered into covenant with God at Mount Sinai (see Exodus 24:3-8).

The Old Testament is loaded with examples of covenants made between two people interacting with each other as contemporaries and friends. An example of this is David and Jonathan who entered into a covenantal relationship because of their love for each other. This concurrence united the both of them and assigned them with very specific responsibilities. *"Then Jonathan and David made a covenant, because he loved him as his own soul"* (1 Sam. 18:3 KJV).

One of the strangest things about God making a covenant with mortal man is the great disparity that exists between the two parties. God is the embodiment of holiness as reflected in His Glory, His Character, and Splendor. Yet this holy God is still desirous of entering into a covenantal relationship with flawed men and women like you and me. And since we are incapable of bridging the tremendous gap between us, God bends down to our level. How could we not jump at such a deal?

It is terribly sad that so many people desire the blessings of the Lord yet so few understand covenant. The great British preacher and pastor of the Metropolitan Tabernacle, Charles Spurgeon, wrote these words for one of his sermons entitled *The Wondrous Covenant* with his text taken from Hebrews 8:10:

> The doctrine of the divine covenant lies at the root of all true theology. It has been said that he who well understands the distinction between the covenant of works and the covenant of grace is a master in divinity. I am persuaded that most of the mistakes which men make concerning the doctrines of Scripture are based upon fundamental errors with regard to the covenants of law and of grace. May God grant us now the power to instruct, and you the grace to receive instruction on this vital subject.[30]

During the same message He clarifies the Christ-Covenant connection that is necessary to make a God-ordained covenant work:

> Having the blessing of the covenant you must needs be in the covenant and being in the covenant Christ evidently must have representatively stood sponsor for you. But saith one, "What is it to believe in Christ?" Another word is a synonym to it. It is—trust Christ. "How do I know whether He died for me in particular?" Trust him whether thou knowest that or not.[31]

The Abrahamic Covenant—A Covenant of Blessings

And said, By myself have I sworn, saith the Lord, for because thou hast done this thing, and hast not withheld thy son,

thine only son: That in blessing I will bless thee, and in mul-
tiplying I will multiply thy seed as the stars of the Heaven,
and as the sand which is upon the sea shore; and thy seed
shall possess the gate of his enemies; and in thy seed shall all
the nations of the earth be blessed; because thou hast obeyed
My voice (Genesis 22:16-18 KJV).

Because Abraham showed the Lord that he was willing to sacrifice his only son Isaac, the very son of his ridiculous promise,
God knew that his heart had been circumcised and that he could
be fully trusted. Often God will *qualify* you just prior to *blessing*
you. He knows that you must be ready for the blessing or you will
not recognize its value. Many Christians, that is many church-
goers, automatically assume that they are deserving of every blessing that God passes out, not taking into account whether they are
actually ready to receive.

Are you ready? Are you? Would you cause the blessing to multiply or would it lose interest through your gross mismanage-
ment? Be honest with yourself. I can give you one major hint: if
you want all of the blessing just for you alone, then you are probably not ready yet. If you, however, realize that God's blessings are
always bigger than our capacity to contain them, then you just
may be on your way.

The Generational Covenant

"And Joseph said unto his brethren, I die: and God will surely
visit you, and bring you out of this land unto the land which he
sware to Abraham, to Isaac, and to Jacob" (Gen. 50:24 KJV). The

wonderful thing about a covenant established by God is that it does not cease—it extends to future generations. God looks at pretty much everything generationally. God doesn't just see Noel Jones; He sees my sons and my sons' sons and their sons. I'm sure you are getting the point. It would be difficult for God to limit His covenantal blessing to just me. For one or more reasons I might disqualify myself from receiving the promise of the covenant. And if I miss my promise, and it stopped with just me— then my heirs would miss it as well.

So if I don't receive the blessing in my lifetime, then what? Consider the African slaves who were promised freedom, yet many of the original slaves never received their freedom. What happened? Did somebody miss it? No, not at all, God thinks generationally. Everything that will come out of you is "you" in the eyes of God. So if you are blessed, you don't have to receive it personally in order for God's Word to be true. Your children and your grandchildren may experience a far better life than you ever dreamed of, all because of God's promise to you. You could be passed over, and the blessing could go to the next generation if you do not fulfill the agreement.

Don't get discouraged so fast. I am not suggesting that you won't receive His blessings in your lifetime. I believe that your time is now and that many of the things that God promised you, you will enjoy. What I am saying is, the things that you may wait for that you never see actualized may be reserved for a generation after you.

Most of the parents of the Gen-Xers thought more about themselves than their offspring—the hottest fashions to wear, the food they wanted to eat, the unrestrained lifestyle they wanted to live. They did not even consider the coming generation. As a result, their children suffered and will continue to suffer until someone stands up, like God, and cries out on their behalf. I've seen bumper stickers that say, "I'm spending my children's inheritance." That may draw a chuckle from those reading it, but it is actually so very sad.

God doesn't give us what belongs to the next generation. If anything, He will do the reverse. Ask God to begin reshaping your mind to think generationally. Think about including your children in on this blessing that you are getting ready to receive. Stretch even further and incorporate the children that have not even arrived on earth yet. They need to have a connection to the covenant from the very day of their birth. That concept, once initiated, will forever change the face of the family, as we now know it. "*A good man leaveth an inheritance to his children's children: and the wealth of the sinner is laid up for the just*" (Prov. 13:22 KJV).

The New Covenant

For when God made promise to Abraham, because He could swear by no greater, He sware by Himself, Saying, Surely blessing I will bless thee, and multiplying I will multiply thee. And so, after he had patiently endured, he obtained the promise (Hebrews 6:13-15 KJV).

For I have received of the Lord that which also I delivered unto you, That the Lord Jesus the same night in which He was betrayed took bread: And when He had given thanks, He brake it, and said, Take, eat: this is My body, which is broken for you: this do in remembrance of Me. After the same manner also He took the cup, when He had supped, saying, This cup is the new testament in My blood: this do ye, as oft as ye drink it, in remembrance of Me. For as often as ye eat this bread, and drink this cup, ye do shew the Lord's death till He come (1 Corinthians 11:23-26 KJV).

One of the highest and most sacred sacraments in the Church of our Lord Jesus Christ is the celebration of the Holy Eucharist. We receive and offer communion to continually reflect on Christ's death, burial, resurrection, and Kingdom reign. Although many churches have made it a habit to perform this rite on the first Sunday of each month, it is just as appropriate to offer this sacrament each and every time we gather together in His name. As often as this sacrament takes place we continue to remember Jesus, which is the whole objective of the sacrament. This was a covenant meal. "*And He took bread, and gave thanks, and brake it, and gave unto them, saying, This is My body which is given for you: this do in remembrance of Me*" (Luke 22:19 KJV).

In this sacrament, too, is a major healing mystery. The blood that was shed on the cross of Christ not only remitted sin, but also sickness and disease. The cup that the Scripture refers to, also known as the new covenant or testament in His blood, speaks of a changing of the guards, a new order if you will. The Old Covenant was not a bad one; as a matter of fact, it was perfect. It was so perfect that no man could live up to it without fail.

That is why Jesus had to come and then become everything that we could not be. What does this have to do with your blessing? It has everything to do with your blessing in that you don't have to work for your blessing, or try to merit a blessing from the Lord. You will receive it because Jesus paid for your blessing. That was a part of the New Covenant. He made possible, through His death and resurrection, for you and I to receive all of the blessings promised us in Scripture. He does not ask us to jump through religious hoops, or dare us to try and follow the Law to the very letter, something that no one could ever do anyhow. You just need to know that Jesus has a track record of blessing people with ridiculous healing, ridiculous favor, ridiculous money, and ridiculous anointing. All you have to do is believe that those ridiculous blessings are really possible in your life.

And Jesus looking upon them saith, With men it is impossible, but not with God: for with God all things are possible (Mark 10:27 KJV).

Chapter 10

It's Worth the Wait

Patience and perseverance have a magical effect before which difficulties disappear and obstacles vanish.[32]

—John Quincy Adams

Have courage for the great sorrows of life and patience for the small ones; and when you have laboriously accomplished your daily task, go to sleep in peace. God is awake.[33]

—Victor Hugo

We live in a society where the character of patience has been lost. We have instant food, instant cash, and instant messaging. While we live in a society that is totally characterized by a lack of patience and an instant gratification mentality, there are many things that will require your patience before they blossom forth. One old axiom that I treasure to this day is,

"Anything that has worth, is worth waiting for." I would add to that bit of wisdom: Anything of lasting value is going to require that you wait. If you choose not to wait, that is obviously your choice. But I want you to know that impatience is tantamount to giving up. And when you choose to throw in the towel, you forfeit all of the rewards you have taken so long to build.

We've talked about how the blessing God has in store for you is so ridiculous that it will, at some point, make you laugh when you find it so much greater than you dared imagine. I can promise you this: your blessing is worth waiting for. Now I'm sure there have been times in your life when you waited quite some time to receive something only to find once it comes, it really was a waste of precious time and energy. And you felt cheated. All that waiting for...what?

No one wants to put great effort to achieve a goal and then come short of reaching that goal. I've watched this happen, particularly in the area of relationships. I've seen a man wait patiently for years for a good woman, believing his time investment will finally pay dividends bringing him the perfect mate—one who will appreciate his kindness, love, and compassion. The devastation he experiences after putting in that kind of time and not reaping the benefit of receiving an equal or greater love as a rate of return is sad to see.

Then there is the woman who has put in lots of overtime loving a man to the best of her ability only to find out that his love was being divided three or four ways. She feels like she has wasted years of her life. Not because they did not share great loving moments, they did. The love was good; the sharing was great, the travel was even better. But those things have nothing to do with the real problem. The bottom line is she feels like she wasted her time because she did not receive what she expected.

There are so many people walking around in this world who have just had their hopes too high. Allow me to help you just a little bit. When you put your unfailing confidence in anyone other than the Lord, you are *going* to be disappointed. I am not suggesting that you should walk through life being totally paranoid. You have to have a level of trust in others just to make it day to day. But you cannot afford to put unfailing confidence in anyone but the Lord. If you do, you are setting yourself up for heartache. "*Trust in the Lord with all thine heart; and lean not unto thine own understanding. In all thy ways acknowledge Him, and He shall direct thy paths*" (Prov. 3:5-6 KJV).

When you've waited and did not get the reward you expected, you begin to believe that waiting is not worth it, even if you are waiting on the Lord. God is not like that at all, let me assure you. You will never wait on God and be disappointed—never. "*God is not a man, that He should lie, nor a son of man, that He should change His mind. Does He speak and then not act? Does He promise and not fulfill?*" (Num. 23:19).

If He promises blessings to you in exchange for a couple of days, months, or years of your time, He'll always make good on His word. So be encouraged. You did not come this far to be left hanging. You are closer than you think!

Has Your Faith Been Tested Yet?

Everybody has faith. "*For I say, through the grace given unto me, to every man that is among you, not to think of himself more highly than he ought to think; but to think soberly, according as God hath dealt to every man the measure of faith*" (Rom. 12:3 KJV). We all have a measure of faith residing within us. But if that faith has never been put to the test, it has not much value to us. However, if you look in that verse above, you will see that faith that has been tested produces the fruit of patience in us, and patience, having done its *perfect* work, will make us mature and complete—*wanting nothing.*

Tertullian, one of the early church fathers, wrote about the connection between faith and patience. "Accordingly it is patience which is both subsequent and antecedent to faith. In short, Abraham believed God, and was accredited by Him with righteousness; but it was patience which *proved* his faith...."[34] You say you have faith and that is a good thing. But the manifestation of your faith must be revealed in your patience.

Before your car came off of the assembly line, it was subjected to a series of tests to prove that the car would withstand all road conditions. It had to be tested under the most extreme of circumstances. It had to go through a rigorous battery of tests to ensure that the vehicle would perform safely and perfectly under every conceivable stress.

Only after the car passed every test perfectly was it shipped out of the factory. In the same way, God is holding you back for just a few more tests. He wants to make sure that when you are connected to your promise and the world sees it that you won't break down, but will perform the way that God engineered you to.

Listen to me, you've waited this long and you've survived. In fact, you are better than ever. You now have an outlook on life that you never would have had, had it not been for all that you endured. You went through your tests, and you have been approved. Now you are ready to seize what is rightfully yours. Your "going through" was not in vain.

God is gonna make you laugh. As you walk in faith with your eyes on the promise, patiently waiting for its fulfillment, joy will come to you. In the end, you will laugh at all that God has done for you. The sorrow of your "waiting moments" will be turned into laughter.

Appendix[35]

University of Maryland School of Medicine Study Shows Laughter Helps Blood Vessels Function Better

What Are the Health Benefits of Humor and Laughter?

The sound of roaring laughter is far more contagious than any cough, sniffle, or sneeze. Humor and laughter can cause a domino effect of joy and amusement, as well as set off a number of positive physical effects. A good hearty laugh can help:

- reduce stress

- lower blood pressure

- elevate mood

- boost immune system

- improve brain functions

- protect the heart

- connect you to others

- foster instant relaxation

- make you feel good

Laughter lowers blood pressure. People who laugh heartily on a regular basis have lower blood pressure than the average person. When people have a good laugh, initially the blood pressure increases, but then it decreases to levels below normal. Breathing then becomes deeper, which sends oxygen-enriched blood and nutrients throughout the body.

Humor changes our biochemical state. Laughter decreases stress hormones and increases infection-fighting antibodies. It increases our attentiveness, heart rate, and pulse.

Laughter protects the heart. Laughter, along with an active sense of humor, may help protect you against a heart attack, according to the study at the University of Maryland Medical Center [cited above]. The study, which is the first to indicate that laughter may help prevent heart disease, found that people with heart disease were 40 percent less likely to laugh in a variety of situations compared to people of the same age without heart disease.

Laughter gives our bodies a good workout. Laughter can be a great workout for your diaphragm, abdominal, respiratory, facial, leg, and back muscles. It massages abdominal organs, tones intestinal functioning, and strengthens the muscles that hold the abdominal organs in place. Not only does laughter give your mid-section a workout; it can benefit digestion and absorption functioning as well. It is estimated that hearty laughter can burn calories equivalent to several minutes on the rowing machine or the exercise bike.

Humor improves brain function and relieves stress. Laughter stimulates both sides of the brain to enhance learning. It eases muscle tension and psychological stress, which keeps the brain alert and allows people to retain more information.

How Does Humor Improve Mental and Emotional Health?

Humor is a powerful emotional medicine that can lower stress, dissolve anger, and unite families in troubled times. Mood is elevated by striving to find humor in difficult and frustrating situations. Laughing at ourselves and the situation helps reveal that small things are not the earth-shaking events they sometimes seem to be. Looking at a problem from a different perspective can make it seem less formidable and provide opportunities for greater objectivity and insight. Humor also helps us avoid loneliness by connecting with others who are attracted to genuine cheerfulness. And the good feeling that we get when we laugh can remain with us as an internal experience even after the laughter subsides.

Why Do We Need Humor to Stay Healthy Emotionally?

A healthy sense of humor is related to being able to laugh at oneself and one's life. Laughing at oneself can be a way of accepting and respecting oneself. Lack of a sense of humor is directly related to lower self-esteem. (Note that laughing at oneself can also be unhealthy if one laughs as a way of self-degradation.)

Humor is essential to mental health for a variety of reasons:

- Humor enhances our ability to affiliate or connect with others.

- Humor helps us replace distressing emotions with pleasurable feelings. You cannot feel angry, depressed, anxious, guilty, or resentful and experience humor at the same time.

- Lacking humor will cause one's thought processes to stagnate, leading to increased distress.

- Humor changes behavior—when we experience humor we talk more, make more eye contact with others, touch others, etc.

- Humor increases energy, and with increased energy we may perform activities that we might otherwise avoid.

- Finally, humor is good for mental health because it makes us feel good!

What Are the Social Benefits of Humor and Laughter?

Our work, marriage, and family all need humor, celebrations, play, and ritual as much as record-keeping and problem-solving. We should ask the questions "Do we laugh together?" as well as "Can we get through this hardship together?" Humor binds us together, lightens our burdens, and helps us keep things in perspective. One of the things that saps our energy is the time, focus, and effort we put into coping with life's problems including each other's limitations. Our families, our friends, and our neighbors are not perfect and neither are our marriages, our kids, or our in-laws. When we laugh together, it can bind us closer together instead of pulling us apart.

Remember that even in the most difficult of times, a laugh, or even simply a smile, can go a long way in helping us feel better.

- Laughter is the shortest distance between two people.

- Humor unites us, especially when we laugh together.

- Laughter heals.

- Laughs and smiles are enjoyed best when shared with others.

- To laugh or not to laugh is your choice.

Endnotes

Introduction

1. www.oprah.com/spiritself/lybl/well/ss_lybl_well_
   health04_e.jhtml.

2 Ibid.

3 www.salwen.com/mtquotes.html.

Chapter 1

4. www.thinkexist.com/quotation/your-time-is-limited-so-don-
   t-waste-it-living/406623.html.

5. Martin Buber, *Tales of the Hasidim* (New York: Schocken
   Books, 1947), 2.

6. www.sillymusic.com/jewish_humor_comedians.asp.

7. www.brainyquote.com/quotes/quotes/m/mayaangelo
    125778.html.

8. www.nonstopenglish.com/reading/quotations/k_
    Anticipation.asp.

Chapter 2

9. www.brainyquote.com/quotes/quotes/w/williamgla
    345833.html.

10. www.motivatingquotes.com/knowledge.htm.

11. www.wisdomquotes.com/001928.html.

Chapter 3

12. www.thinkexist.com/quotation/god_whispers_to_us_in_
    our_pleasures-speaks_to_us/180233.html.

13. www.quotegarden.com/change.html.

14. www.thinkexist.com/quotation/when_you_have_come_
    to_the_edge_of_all_light_that/173385.html.

Chapter 4

15. www.answers.com/topic/buckham-james.

16. www.thinkexist.com/quotation/character_cannot_be_
    developed_in_ease_and_quiet/13579.html.

17. www.poemhunter.com/poem/the-hollow-men/

Chapter 5

18. www.friendship.com.au/quotes/quofri.html.

19. www.sfgate.com/cgi-bin/article.cgi?file=/chronicle/ archive/2004/01/29/MNGC74KEA71.DTL.

Chapter 6

20. www.brainyquote.com/quotes/authors/w/warren_buffett.html

21. John Maxwell, *The Winning Attitude: Your Key to Personal Success* (Nashville: Thomas Nelson Publishers, 1993), 90.

22. Victor Frankl, *Man's Search for Meaning* (New York: Washington Square Press, 1985), 104.

Chapter 7

23. www.acadisc.com/revivalif.htm#jesus.

24. www.negrospirituals.com/news-song/nobody_ know_de_trouble_i_ve_seen.htm.

25. Paul Tillich, *Systematic Theology, Vol. 1* (Chicago: University of Chicago Press, 1973), 211.

26. S.D. Gordon, *Quiet Talks About Jesus* (Shippensburg, PA: Destiny Image Publishers, 2003), 15, originally published in 1903.

Chapter 8

27. www.afroamhistory.about.com/od/dukeellington/a/ quotes_elling_d.htm.

28. www.thinkexist.com/quotation/the_hardest_arithmetic_
to_master_is_that_which/204398.html.

29. www.thinkexist.com/quotation/reflect_upon_your_
present_blessings__of_which/176511.html.

Chapter 9

30. Spurgeon's Sermons, Electronic Database. Copyright 1997 by
Biblesoft.

31. Ibid.

Chapter 10

32. www.wisdomquotes.com/cat_patience.html.

33. www.quotationspage.com/quote/2452.html.

34. www.newadvent.org/fathers/0325.htm.

Appendix

35. www.umm.edu/news/releases/laughter2.html?source
=google.

Notes

_____

_____

_____

_____

_____

_____

_____

_____

_____

_____

_____

_____

_____

_____

_____

_____

_____

_____

_____

_____

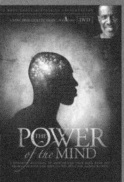

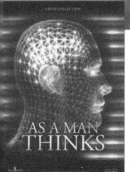

FAITHMATE™
DATING FOR FAITHFUL LIFESTYLES

FaithMate.com is designed for single and previously married urban Christians that are seeking meaningful relationships.

At FaithMate.com, no more uneasy pick-up lines in church. All you need is our PROPRIETARY MATCHING SYSTEM to profile, recommend and connect you with that special someone that the Lord may have just for you.

Find your faith mate today at www.FaithMate.com

When it comes to online dating, all you need is faith, all you need is ...

FAITHMATE™.COM
DATING FOR FAITHFUL LIFESTYLES

Additional copies of this book and other
book titles from DESTINY IMAGE are
available at your local bookstore.

Call toll free: 1-800-722-6774.

Send a request for a catalog to:

Destiny Image₍₎ Publishers, Inc.
P.O. Box 310
Shippensburg, PA 17257-0310

*"Speaking to the Purposes of God for this
Generation and for the Generations to Come."*

**For a complete list of our titles,
visit us at www.destinyimage.com**